10 MESSAGES
YOUR ANGELS
WANT YOU
TO KNOW

Also by Doreen Virtue

Books/Kits/Oracle Board

Awaken Your Indigo Power (with Charles Virtue)

Veggie Mama (with Jenny Ross)

The Courage to Be Creative

Nutrition for Intuition (with Robert Reeves, N.D.)

Don't Let Anything Dull Your Sparkle

Earth Angel Realms

Living Pain-Free (with Robert Reeves, N.D.)

The Big Book of Angel Tarot (with Radleigh Valentine)

Angels of Abundance (with Grant Virtue)

Angel Dreams (with Melissa Virtue)

Angel Astrology 101 (with Yasmin Boland)

Angel Detox (with Robert Reeves, N.D.)

Assertiveness for Earth Angels

How to Heal a Grieving Heart (with James Van Praagh)

The Essential Doreen Virtue Collection

The Miracles of Archangel Gabriel

Mermaids 101

Flower Therapy (with Robert Reeves, N.D.)

Mary, Queen of Angels

Saved by an Angel

The Angel Therapy® Handbook

Angel Words (with Grant Virtue)

Archangels 101

The Healing Miracles of Archangel Raphael

The Art of Raw Living Food (with Jenny Ross)

The Miracles of Archangel Michael

Angel Numbers 101

Solomon's Angels (a novel)

My Guardian Angel (with Amy Oscar)

Angel Blessings Candle Kit (with Grant Virtue; includes booklet, CD, journal, etc.)

Thank You, Angels! (children's book with Kristina Tracy)

Healing Words from the Angels

How to Hear Your Angels

Signs from Above (with Charles Virtue)

Fairies 101

Daily Guidance from Your Angels

Divine Magic

How to Give an Angel Card Reading Kit

Angels 101

Angel Guidance Board

Crystal Therapy (with Judith Lukomski)

Connecting with Your Angels Kit (includes booklet, CD, journal, etc.)

The Crystal Children

Archangels & Ascended Masters

Earth Angels

Messages from Your Angels

Angel Visions II

Eating in the Light (with Becky Black, M.F.T., R.D.)

The Care and Feeding of Indigo Children

Angel Visions

Divine Prescriptions

Healing with the Angels

"I'd Change My Life If I Had More Time"

Divine Guidance

Chakra Clearing

Angel Therapy®

Constant Craving A–Z

Constant Craving

The Yo-Yo Diet Syndrome

Losing Your Pounds of Pain

Audio/CD Programs

Don't Let Anything Dull Your Sparkle (unabridged audio book)

The Healing Miracles of Archangel Raphael
(unabridged audio book)

Angel Therapy® Meditations
Archangels 101 (abridged audio book)
Solomon's Angels (unabridged audio book)
Fairies 101 (abridged audio book)
Angel Medicine (available as both 1- and 2-CD sets)
Angels among Us (with Michael Toms)
Messages from Your Angels (abridged audio book)
Past-Life Regression with the Angels
Divine Prescriptions
The Romance Angels
Connecting with Your Angels
Manifesting with the Angels
Karma Releasing
Healing Your Appetite, Healing Your Life
Healing with the Angels
Divine Guidance
Chakra Clearing

DVD Program

How to Give an Angel Card Reading

Calendar

Angel Affirmations (for each individual year)

Card Decks

Butterfly Oracle Cards for Life Changes
Loving Words from Jesus
Fairy Tarot Cards (with Radleigh Valentine)
Archangel Gabriel Oracle Cards
Angel Answers Oracle Cards (with Radleigh Valentine)
Past Life Oracle Cards (with Brian Weiss, M.D.)

All of the above are available at your local bookstore, or may be ordered through Hay House USA: www.hayhouse.com®; Hay House Australia: www.hayhouse.com.au; Hay House UK: www.hayhouse.co.uk; Hay House South Africa: www.hayhouse.co.za; Hay House India: www.hayhouse.co.in

Doreen's website: www.AngelTherapy.com

10 MESSAGES
YOUR ANGELS
WANT YOU
TO KNOW

Doreen Virtue

HAY HOUSE, INC.
Carlsbad, California • New York City
London • Sydney • Johannesburg
Vancouver • New Delhi

Published and distributed in the United States by: Hay House, Inc.: www
.hayhouse.com® • *Published and distributed in Australia by:* Hay House
Australia Pty. Ltd.: www.hayhouse.com.au • *Published and distributed in
the United Kingdom by:* Hay House UK, Ltd.: www.hayhouse.co.uk • *Pub-
lished and distributed in the Republic of South Africa by:* Hay House SA
(Pty), Ltd.: www.hayhouse.co.za • *Distributed in Canada by:* Raincoast
Books: www.raincoast.com • *Published in India by:* Hay House Publishers
India: www.hayhouse.co.in

Cover and interior design: Nick C. Welch

Cataloging-in-Publication Data
is on file with the Library of Congress

ISBN: 978-1-4019-5401-7

10 9 8 7 6 5 4 3 2 1

1st edition, May 2017

SUSTAINABLE
FORESTRY
INITIATIVE

Certified Sourcing
www.sfiprogram.org
SFI-01268

SFI label applies to text stock only

Ethically printed in the United States of America

Contents

Introduction

What the Angels Want You to Know

This book has been a long time coming to fruition.

As a very small child, I sensed the presence of angels without knowing what I was seeing, hearing, or experiencing. All I knew was that whenever I felt upset, beings of light would come to comfort me. They calmed my sensitive heart and reassured me that I was loved and safe.

They also taught me many things—lessons that I'm excited to share with you—about how life can be "Heavenly" right now.

The angels are guardians to you and me, and the term *angel* means "messenger of God." There are many beings in the spirit world who deliver messages, but not all of them are trustworthy or in the Divine light. I've learned discernment, and practiced spiritual protection, to ensure that I'm only speaking with true angels of God.

You can distinguish a true angel from a lower being by some hallmark characteristics. True angels . . .

- . . . are entirely giving and generous, without asking for anything in return.

- . . . are like God in all ways: loving, wise, compassionate, and forgiving.

- . . . never tire—because, like God, they have unlimited energy.

- . . . can be with everyone simultaneously, as they have pure energy bodies, not limited physical bodies.

Sometimes people think of their departed loved ones as angels. And while loved ones in Heaven can be helpful like an angel, they still have human egos (which true angels do not).

As a lifelong sensitive intuitive, I've seen that every person has two or more guardian angels with them at all times, usually stationed next to each shoulder. As you'll read in this book, they are governed by God's Law of Free Will with respect to the choices we make. That's why tragedy and evil can exist, when people make freewill choices to act in ways that are hurtful.

The messages in this book discuss reality from the perspectives of both duality and nonduality, because the angels can see both the real and the illusory worlds:

- *Duality* is the illusory world where it appears that we are all separated from one another, and it can feel like God is far away and perhaps isn't hearing or answering our prayers.

- The world of *nonduality* is the real world God created. It means the complete awareness of—and respect for—the fact that you and I are one with God, the angels, and each other.

The angels address both perspectives, because we tend to vacillate between both worlds.

I'm often asked why I talk with angels instead of with God or Jesus. The answer is that I *do* talk with God and

Jesus constantly, and I highly recommend that others do so also. Messages from the angels are the collective voice of God's messages (which are one with Holy Spirit, Jesus, and our higher self), delivered to us by the Heavenly messengers. Because angels have no egos, their messages are purely from God.

As you'll read in this book, God's vantage point of 100 percent pure love is a very high vibration. In fact, pure love is the *highest* possible vibration.

We can attain this vibration through having an open heart, praying, meditating, forgiving, connecting with nature, and so forth. This is when you feel a sense of oneness and of loving everyone with all your soul.

Such moments can be fleeting, though, as the "real world" pulls us down to a lower vibration where we judge ourselves or others. This leads to seeing ourselves as separated, which in turn brings up loneliness and emotional pain.

That's where the angels come in. They bridge the nonduality and duality worlds that we vacillate between. The angels can reach us and teach us, no matter how stressed, judgmental, or afraid we are.

Some of the messages in this book may cover knowledge that you already have, and serve as helpful reminders. I personally learned a lot while receiving the messages in this book, and discovered new perspectives and practical guidance.

This book can also give you guidance if you open it to a random page. Whatever you read upon doing so is a personalized message for you.

The rest of the book after this Introduction is entirely in the voice of the angels, exactly as I received their messages. Just like my earlier books *Angel Therapy* and *Messages from Your Angels*, *10 Messages Your Angels Want You to Know* was dictated to me by the angels after I asked for their guidance. They chose the topics, and they told me exactly what to write. In my earlier books, the angels explained answers to my questions about life and the world. In this book, I didn't ask any questions, because the angels had a complete thesis to share. I simultaneously hear their collective voice in my ears while also receiving visions and intellectual downloads of information.

Interestingly, I paid my college tuition by working as a secretary for many years. As such, I'd type letters that my bosses dictated into a tape machine. When I type messages from the angels, I feel like a *Heavenly* secretary. Just like I would transcribe recordings while putting myself through school, I type the messages I receive exactly as I hear them, without any of my own opinions or thoughts. It's pure dictation, and you'll feel the high vibration of the angels' messages as you read them.

My prayer is that reading this book will help you develop an even clearer connection with your own Divine guidance. May the messages in these pages open you to hearing God's personal messages for *you*.

With love and respect,

Doreen

1

The Waking Dream

A Message about Your True Identity

Dear One, we begin these messages by assuring you of our complete respect for the difficulties you face as a human persona. We have the utmost compassion in acknowledging the challenges that you endure. We watch the human struggles, and do our best to intervene as we are invited to do so. It is our endeavor to awaken ancient memories within you, to guide you on your way back home.

We have nothing new to teach or share, only these reminders of what you already know within your soul. For we are of the same substance as you: creations of the Divine Creator.

We are the messengers of the Creator, the very thought-forms from God, desiring to reach you and awaken you to the happy truths. These dawning realizations enable you to experience a happier dream, as well. For it is true that "life is but a dream," which we will help you understand in practical terms with applications that you will say "improve" your life.

As you read our words, we are also individually connecting with you. You'll hear a second narrative within your mind and feelings as you read our words here. This will awaken realizations that have been previously blocked from conscious awareness.

You have asked us to accelerate your spiritual learning, and we will move you along as quickly as you feel comfortable. You are always and ultimately in charge of this process.

We can see the duality and oneness of you, simultaneously—although duality is but a very realistic dream we call "adventures of the ego." Therefore, we see the *you* who is dreaming a story of being alone and often feeling frustrated and abandoned. A dreaming you who wonders where God is, and why your prayers aren't being answered.

We see everything in your beingness, from the lowest to the highest vibrations, all occurring at once. For you have increasingly conscious memories of the true you in what you would call "Heaven," which is a state of being that we will explain further to you.

You remember being limitless. You remember how everything immediately reacted to your thoughts and feelings. You remember unconditional love so intense that your soul yearns for the same experience of merging with others.

Sometimes at night your soul travels back to your Heavenly origins. There, you reconnect with your soul family, as well as educators who teach classes in the crystalline temples. Your spiritual heart opens wide, because you feel entirely safe there. No ego, no body, and nothing to protect. You are home.

And then you awaken, ironically, back into the waking dream many call "reality." You vaguely recall your dream visitations, with a longing to return. Even more, you wish to remember the profound truths and connections made during the dream visit. Yet, the visions and truths given to you in the multidimensional world make no sense in the three-dimensional waking world. So your conscious mind blocks them until some experience triggers ancient memories.

Mostly what you are craving is that feeling of complete acceptance and belonging you experience in the Heavenly world. There is no struggle to "prove yourself" or any concerns about worthiness, for everyone's light shines equally brilliantly. Love is a constant waterfall of abundance, so competition does not exist.

And this is what you remember, perhaps on an increasingly conscious level. In the waking world, you have moments mirroring these pleasures. Perhaps a glass of wine, a piece of chocolate, a romantic date, or a career accomplishment gives you the fleeting feeling you are seeking.

Even longer lasting are the deep relationships between parent and baby, with all of the hopes elevated and the worries in the distance. You may also experience the pure connection of oneness with an animal companion, in a peaceful partnership, or while gazing at a sunset from a mountain plateau.

Your overriding instinctual drive isn't for food or power, but for merging with love. You crave complete acceptance, which includes completely accepting yourself.

When you don't feel completely accepted, you tend to blame yourself. You may worry about social shortcomings and overcompensate by trying to impress others, thereby distracting yourself from . . . yourself.

Or you may blame the other person, which usually is a way to defend against hurt feelings. The truth is that the doorway from Heaven to Earth is so filled with pressure that most people close their hearts as an automatic reaction of fear. We liken it to the atmosphere change when you descend quickly in an airplane, or even underwater. There's a heaviness that comes from descending into the dense physical environment, and it feels as if everything is clumsy and awkward . . . including you.

The theme of Earth is "incompleteness," which is ironic since God created you complete. This includes your having the complete power to fulfill the earthly needs of your body.

From parents, you learn of the need to protect yourself from perceived dangers and to compete for and chase after fulfillment of your material needs.

And yet, as we are here to teach and guide you, everything that you need is already with you as a thought-form that rapidly materializes. This will be an *un*learning for you, and a remembering of what you knew prior to your earthly incarnation.

So, let's take you back to your soul origins, to help you remember who you are, your true identity, and why you're here.

Who Is God?

The traditional view of God is an elderly man in the sky, seated upon a throne. The personalization of God helps some feel a closer bond, similar to having a beloved uncle who is an excellent listener and extremely helpful and supportive.

Viewing God as a faraway man is one of the origins of "separation thinking," according to which humans are in the dense earthly environment and God and the angels are in the lofty clouds of Heaven. These anthropomorphic projections were originally a way of explaining Earth experiences such as storms, earthquakes, and fires. Romantic stories about pleased or displeased gods and deities helped humans feel more in control.

From there began superstitious rituals to appease God and influence the dispensation of Divine protection and favors. Cause-and-effect observations created lore. For example, if someone performed a specific planting ceremony and then the next day the seedlings sprouted through the ground, that ceremony was thought to be the cause and the good crops the effects.

Because God's creation energy *does* yield desirable results, beliefs solidified about how to please and influence God. Religions and texts were formed around these beliefs as a way of sharing what worked and what didn't work. At its basic core, this dogma is a very loving act of teaching others how to receive God's blessings.

Yet, as you know, religion can become a reflection of a denser energy of fear. If a religion teaches fear as a way of pleasing God, then people are actually being pushed away from their conscious awareness of God's love.

The truth lies somewhere in the middle, as there are certain guidelines for living and lifestyle that will help someone feel closer to God. For example, having a clear and quiet mind, without impedances of worry, anger, or chemicals, definitely makes it easier to comprehend the wavelength of God's messages.

It's not that God is displeased with a certain lifestyle, as God is 100 percent love, with not one space for anything less than love. If you think of a circle, with everything inside it being pure, then there is no room for impurity. If the circle contains *only* pure love, then it cannot also simultaneously contain judgment, fear, anger, or anything else considered "negative."

God, being pure love, has no judgment, fear, anger, or negativity. Teachings about an angry God are based upon beliefs that God destroys in vengeance. This was how your ancestors felt in control, by explaining why crops failed or natural disasters occurred. Although they were afraid of future destruction by a "punishing God," they also felt they could avoid these problems by making sacrifices to God.

Originally, sacrifice was literal bloodshed of animals and sometimes people, as a way of "giving" something to God in exchange for mercy. With today's under-standing, blood sacrifices seem like primitive and need-less cruelties. However, this ancient superstition about sacrifice has morphed into modern-day self-sacrificing behavior, such as denying your basic emotional and physical needs.

There's a belief that others (including God) would feel sorry for your suffering and spare you. This belief is reinforced in human relationships, where suffering is rewarded with sympathy, disability payments, lawsuit settlements, and receiving care from others.

Sometimes the sacrificial suffering is done silently and secretly. This is similar to herd animals who are ban-ished if they reveal they are sick, because of the herd's self-preservation instinct to avoid the spread of conta-gious illnesses between animals. Animals who are subject to being prey also hide their illness or injuries so as not to appear weak.

So, too, do humans twist the way in which they deal with their personal suffering. Some people proudly wear their suffering, like a martyr exclaiming, "Look at all that

I've done for you!" while others hide it out of shame or not wanting to burden others.

Hiding or ignoring suffering can slightly lessen its impact, as it is true that whatever you focus upon does grow in size and strength. However, suffering silently alone can also prolong the time the pain is endured. Asking for, and accepting, help from others—including from us angels—can reduce the amount and duration of pain.

And yet, we witness people rejecting this pathway of peace, because they doubt whether they deserve happiness. So let's discuss your deservingness next.

Deservingness and Confidence

As we continually reiterate, God created you. God, the magnificent and all-encompassing Creator of the universe, made *you*.

Everything and everyone created by God is deliberate. There are no accidents or "factory seconds." Everything and everyone is precisely created for a specific reason and purpose.

God didn't reach for random parts to make you. You were created *from* God and *by* God. Therefore, the substance of all of you is from and by God.

Everyone and everything is not only from God but *in* God. The far reaches of the twists and folds of the universe are inside of God. The tiniest quark and atom are inside of God. *You* are inside of God, along with every other person, animal, bird, fish, and tree that share the same home with you. This is a home that extends far beyond the reaches of a mere planet. This is a home within the mind and heart of God, and it's where you are right now as you read these words.

So, you currently reside within the power of God.

You live within the love of God.

You are, right now, within the health of God.

You presently are in the wisdom and intelligence of God.

Your entire being rests in God.

There is no part of you that is separate or away from God.

Since God is continuously exuding and being the state of pure unconditional love, you are perpetually bathed in the highest frequency of love. You literally live in Heaven right now!

If it doesn't feel that way, this is a sign of walking upon a lower-vibrational pathway of fear. Most humans walk upon this pathway, and encourage others to do so as well. The daily dramas all perpetuate fear, and awareness of these dramas is considered to be a human sign of intelligence.

Not only will we help you to choose the pathway of love—we will dissolve the pathway of fear for you so that it's no longer an option.

The analogy of a pathway is not entirely accurate, either, for it implies that you are traveling or progressing somewhere. How could one who already lives within the supreme knowledge, love, and wisdom need to travel, grow, or progress? Only in the dreamlike illusion of inadequacy and separation, like a nightmare where you attempt to run away from a monster or find your way back home after getting lost. When you awaken, you realize that there are no monsters and you're already home.

Confidence is not about your individual identity, but about who you are and where you live. You *are* the creation of the Creator, Who—like any loving parent—wills that all of your needs be met.

You feel and hear the thoughts of God, which are translated into human action steps for you to take. Perhaps some of these steps lead to a fulfilling career or another condition supportive of your loving pathway.

When God relays a Divine assignment for you, you can be sure that you have been hand selected and will be told exactly how to fulfill this mission. As long as you are listening and following, there is no possibility of "failure." Your successful mission is assured.

Trust and have faith in God's Divine directions, which always lead you along the pathway of love.

The term *deservingness* may imply that one person is more deserving than the other, which is a fear-based thought of separation. Yet, the spiritual truth of this concept stems from the analogy of the sun continuously emitting rays of light. Do the plants argue whether they "deserve" to receive the sunlight? No, because they need the light. And so do you.

When you receive support from God in the form of beautiful experiences and your needs being met, you are a plant gratefully drinking in the sunlight. This allows you to be strong and share your strength with others.

In this regard, deservingness is not solely about you receiving on an individual basis. It is not about selfishness. Deservingness more accurately means allowing yourself to receive all of the uplifting love God is continuously exuding. And as you receive, so do you inspire, uplift, and help others, too. The more you allow yourself to receive, the more you can give.

Suffering Is Physically but Not Spiritually Real

Let us now return to the discussion of your Creator and the true nature of you and the world you experience. . . .

We have agreed that God is pure love, with no room for anything negative. Many have asked the logical question of where God is, in the midst of human suffering. "Why didn't God prevent or heal this?" is a cry we often hear, and wish to answer now.

First, we realize that this passage may offend or shock some, but it is the spiritual truth. Please read this entire section to understand it:

God does not see or know about suffering.

This is because God is pure love, and can only know and see pure love. Any knowledge of suffering would imply that a part of God is less than pure love, which is impossible.

God all-knowingly sees you and everyone as you truly are: a brilliant being of pure Divine love, and every good aspect of love. Therefore, you are strong, powerful, wise, intelligent, creative, lovable, abundant, healthy, balanced, and so forth.

Your true self, also known as your higher self, is 100 percent merged and one with God. So your true self doesn't experience or see suffering either. This is not to say that suffering or pain isn't physically real, as we angels can see these entanglements. Suffering is not spiritually real, but it is physically real, and you will see how understanding this distinction leads to healing, protection, and peace.

All of the suffering of this world is from the opposite of God: fear, and its attributes of guilt, jealousy, competitiveness, perception of lack, and so forth. This is a form of forgetfulness, in which humans forget the pure love power that is their true identity. They then begin to take action from a place of helplessness and powerlessness.

The Dream of Fear

Of course, in spiritual truth, it is impossible for God's creations to be helpless or powerless. God gave you and everyone the same and equally complete spiritual gifts, which are akin to what you'd call "superpowers," as they allow you to create as God creates through focused intention.

In fact, we angels and the Holy Spirit are the "bridges" between God's pure love consciousness (which is also your true self's pure love consciousness) and the world of suffering and separation. We can see both the spiritual and the physical realities of the manifestations of love and fear.

We angels are sent as intermediaries to uplift your vibrations toward the highest levels. While we—like you—are one with God's highest and purest vibration of love, we can enter into the nightmare of separation. Like the interval colors within the rainbow, we are able to blend into the dense vibrations to connect you with the higher vibrations.

This is why it's sometimes easier to feel or hear an angel or the Holy Spirit, and God can feel far away. The only reason for that experience is that your focus upon fear creates a lower vibration, which doesn't consciously connect with the highest vibration of pure love.

When you become ensnared in fearful thoughts or feelings, God seems distant. This is akin to a child panicking from being separated from a parent. Yet God is never far away, since God is omnipresent (meaning "everywhere"). God is within you, and within every person and situation. That means pure love is within you, within everyone, and within every situation.

There is not one tiny, small space where God's pure love doesn't exist, except in the dream of fear. And since the dream isn't real in spiritual truth, fear doesn't exist either.

What about the fear of mortal danger or not having your physical needs met? These are bodily concerns that we will discuss with you. For now, though, know that your true self has no worries, fears, or concerns about protecting or feeding your body. All of those worries are from your lower self.

We angels and the Holy Spirit are able to descend into the dream of fear, to rescue you and bring you back up to your true self's pure love consciousness. We are the knights of God, sent on a mission to keep you centered in your true self and to waken you from nightmares of pain, suffering, victimhood, and other aspects of fear.

2

Why 2 + 2 ≠ 3

A Message about Free Will

You may have heard that fears are self-fulfilling, and this is partially true. However, one aspect that needs explaining is that fear—being unreal—does not have any true creative power. Only what God created can create.

So a fearful focus can appear to create a fearful experience, but what's really occurring is that a fearful consciousness is an *unconsciousness*. Without the awareness of love in your focus, your life is like a ship without a captain at the wheel. The surrounding currents will push it away from its intended destination.

In our analogy, these currents would be the fearful energies of your own thoughts and the thoughts of others. So it's not that you are creating or attracting painful circumstances, as your Divine power of creation cannot create anything but extensions of love. It's just that a lack of awareness of love leaves you open to the influence of fearful energies. Again, like the drifting-ship analogy.

Now, you may correctly ask, *How, if love truly is all-pervasive, can someone focus upon something other than love?*

This brings us to the nature of the physical world, which we will explore very soon. For now, we'd like to stay focused upon your personal true identity. Let's begin this discussion by examining the concept of "free will."

The Truth about Free Will

Most people think of free will as the ability to make their own decisions. Indeed, you've likely heard that God gave people free will, and the reason for suffering is that God cannot intervene into someone's freewill choices without their consent. This is an accurate yet simplistic way of understanding free will.

Here's the more detailed explanation: Free will means that you are either creating from love in the real world or creating in the dream world of that which does not last. So you can create temporary experiences, which you may consider exciting, by creating within the dream. But as soon as you awaken, the dream figures and creations evaporate back to where they came from: nowhere. This creates a feast-or-famine roller-coaster experience, where one moment you're elated and the next moment you're worried.

Freewill choices really mean that you can choose which aspect of love to focus upon. Just as the various colors all make up the rainbow, so are there different variations of love such as gratitude, appreciation, compassion, and nurturing.

When you choose to focus upon love, you create real and lasting creations that are meaningful and filled with blessings for you and others. You are the sun shining rays of light to warm and illuminate others.

The love choice is the highest vibration, which in turn connects you with the highest-vibrational ideas and insights. You receive "downloads" of brilliant ideas and epiphanies, as well as practical ideas and guidance to help you in everyday life.

Why Prayers Seem to Not Be Answered

Another aspect of free will in need of further explaining is why some prayers seem to be unanswered. Most commonly, we see this human frustration when someone prays for a loved one's health.

It's essential to understand that the decisions a person makes about their health and life span are very personal. These are freewill decisions, based upon many levels of factors.

When a person is in a serious health crisis, their consciousness is already in Heaven with us, like a perpetual dream state. In these dream-consciousness moments, we show the person their various options. They not only see but experience what it would be like to choose recovery, passing into Heaven, and other avenues.

They experience ahead of time how these choices will affect their loved ones. For example, a person who has been in a serious accident will experience and decide whether it's better living with a disability and risking affecting their family's lifestyle or passing away physically and risking their family's grief. Each person weighs these options, with the help of their Heavenly companions.

Rest assured that no decision to live or pass away is ever undertaken lightly. If someone is determined to stay, this will happen—and that's when people proclaim that their prayers were answered. Prayers give the person the strength to choose to stay, and fervent prayers also help them realize the depth of their family's love.

All prayers are heard, felt, and received. When you pray for someone else's health, it blankets them with the warm energy of love . . . provided that your prayers are purely for the other person's well-being.

Just like with giving, prayers can be motivated by either love or fear. So, if you are praying for a person's health because you don't want that person to suffer and you care about their happiness and life purpose, this is a love-based prayer that will lift them up. However, if you pray about their health because you are afraid of the consequences for yourself, this is a fear-based prayer.

Always, what you give is what you receive. So it can seem that prayers are ignored only because low-vibrational prayers stay in the low vibrations of the Earth plane. This is akin to forcing something to happen. You can try to squeeze out or chase a miracle, but the results will be a material-illusion mirage, and won't be satisfying or long lasting.

So how do you pray for yourself with selfless love? What if you really need something? Is that egoic, fear-based praying?

These are valid questions that we will explore next.

Prayer from Love-Based Intentions

As with giving to others, giving to yourself originates with an identical choice of the path of love or fear. So it is with praying for yourself.

As you pray, be very aware of your intentions behind your prayers. *Why* are you praying for this? If it's a fear-based reason, you will recognize that you believe you are lacking something that can be fulfilled externally. For example, if you believe that you lack happiness and pray for an object or situation to give you happiness, this prayer cannot be answered. Prayers can appear blocked or delayed at times not because God is "withholding" or because of a universal block, but because of focus taking a detour away from love.

It's the equivalent of demanding that 2 plus 2 equal 3. No matter how much you beg God and make sacrifices, 2 plus 2 can never equal 3. Praying for an external reward to equate to happiness, fulfillment, or peace can never add up. And because it won't add up, you may believe that your plea is ignored, and you may feel stuck. As you can see from the arithmetic example, your prayers aren't being ignored. They just don't compute.

The same lack of results occurs when you outline *how* you wish your prayers to be answered. For instance, if you desire to move into a new home, you may pray to win the lottery to pay for it. This is essentially handing God a script of how you expect everything to work out.

The fear in this scenario manifests as a lack of trust in God's infinite wisdom (which is one with your true self's wisdom). There's a fear that you won't get help with your housing needs unless you give God ideas on how to fulfill this prayer.

The path of love in praying for yourself is filled with gratitude and faith in God providing for your earthly needs. It's a joyous *Hallelujah!* at knowing that God is moving you somewhere wonderful, where your services will bring blessings to others.

With love-based prayer, you have complete faith in God's wisdom to take care of all of the details. And since God's mind is merged with yours, you immediately receive guidance if your actions are needed. For example, you may have a strong feeling to drive down a certain street. As you follow this guidance—*voilà!*—you find a wonderful home in your price range.

Let's say that you are Divinely guided to be a healer. Perhaps you have already practiced healing work on friends, with pets, or professionally. You experience great joy and a sense of timelessness whenever you're engaged in anything having to do with healing. This is a love-based intention.

However, if you doubt your calling to do healing, you have veered off the path of love. You may unconsciously look for external ways to validate your healing abilities, such as deciding—on your own, because of insecurities—that you need to have a "healing center," be published, hold a degree, or receive some other external validation, before you are able to be the healer God is guiding you to be.

Such prayers are not answered like a genie granting your wish—because they are, again, like asking for 2 plus 2 to equal 3.

The only type of prayer that is heard is a love-based intention, where you joyfully intend to share your joy, light, healing energy, and other assets with others.

Now, opening a healing center, publishing a book, and earning a degree are only fear-based paths if you desire them *because* of fears. In contrast, if you are joyfully guided toward these endeavors, this is your love-based path. Even with a love-based path, you may still encounter insecurities and self-doubts. The key is how you handle those fears: internally, such as listening to your inner voice and taking measures to calm yourself, or externally, by deciding to have an "accomplishment" prop up your ego.

The path of love is centered internally, while the road of fear always looks for external solutions. You may *feel* our words as we convey these differences between love and fear to you. The higher vibration of love is always harmonious, like a beautiful melody. Love feels warm, safe, and caressing, while the path of fear feels "off," as if something is wrong.

So, returning to our healing example, a love-based prayer would be along the lines of asking God for Divine assignments to provide healing services. You have faith that God knows exactly who could be matched with your healing energy, and the best place for healings to occur. You trust that if someone comes to you for a healing, God sent that person. These healings may take place in an informal setting, because *where* doesn't matter. You also have no concerns about financial remuneration for your healing work, because you know that as long as you walk through the doors God opens for you, all of your earthly needs are met.

This does not mean that God will give you riches, as a love-based path usually entails simplicity. Of course, you will be provided with a safe and comfortable place to live and everything that you need (not want) for your Divinely guided work. But fancy externals designed to impress others are always from a fear-based path, which is not something God wills for you.

If you live beyond your financial means in order to acquire something that you believe will impress others, this is a lower-vibrational pathway—and that always leads to more experiences of lack and often pain and drama.

The lower pathways of fear and insecurity can never connect you to the higher pathways you desire to walk. The pathway of fear never leads to what you're seeking. It always promises happiness, but instead delivers emptiness and loneliness. Externals are mirages and illusions with hollow energy.

Forgive yourself if you've succumbed to the pathway of fear. Most people have. As long as you're *aware* of its effects, then it has been a useful learning experience.

So with your love-based path, your entire focus is upon joyfully following your intuitive messages and sharing your God-given gifts as you are guided—immersed in love instead of insecurity, guilt, obligation, competition, or other forms of fear.

Blessings on the Path of Love

Perhaps one of the most appreciated benefits of your love focus is that you stop doubting yourself and your ideas. You have supreme confidence in the validity of the high-vibrational ideas, and complete faith that you will be led—one step at a time—to bring them to fruition.

Contrast this loving focus with a fear-based focus, which usually begins with wanting something predicated upon the belief of being separate from God and others. For example, you may feel insecure socially and believe others are judging or avoiding you. So you try to compensate by building yourself up with something that makes you feel "special."

Well, "special" is the same as "separated," and both conditions lead to deep loneliness, as you feel isolated from God and other people. You become "homesick for Heaven," where your soul remembers the delicious sense of safety, security, and merged oneness with all. You frantically begin to seek these Heavenly feelings, and are frustrated that they are fleeting and elusive. You long to connect with God, other people, and the feeling of being loved.

The fear-based approach says that if you can get people to admire you, like you, or be envious of you, then you will feel those same Heavenly feelings. So you work hard to afford the best home, clothing, and cars and to earn college degrees and other accolades. And perhaps there *is* a feeling of accomplishment and pride.

And, yes, people may in fact be attracted to you. It's likely, though, that they're attracted to what they believe you can do for them. They, too, are lost and feeling separated from their Source, and have forgotten their God-given identity and power. So they are looking for outside "sources" and gravitate to one who seems to have power, prestige, abundance, and so forth.

Here is God's truth: Nothing in this material world will ever make you permanently happy. Nothing external leads to internal happiness. Facing this realization can make you depressed at first. But then you get happy, because the chase is over. The expensive, time-consuming, distracting chase for happiness has finally come to an end.

Trying to win or buy other people's approval only pulls you away from a loving focus that can lead to truly satisfying and harmonious relationships. If someone is judging you, that is their low-vibrational freewill choice. To judge them in return or try to gain their approval is to meet them on the low-vibrational path.

Instead of *low*-vibrational, be *love*-vibrational. Go back to your basics about everyone's true, fundamental spiritual identity. Refuse to walk the low-vibrational path! Get up on the higher roads by focusing upon God's reality. See only love in yourself and others, and the fear-based relationships will either heal or drop away. Either you will inspire others and pull them up to the love vibration or—if their freewill choice is otherwise—they will meet upon the path of fear.

We angels enter as characters into your dream of being cast away upon a planet filled with danger and cold, uncaring strangers. Within the dream, we carry you back to the awareness of your Heavenly home with God. You still remain within the physical body; however, the shift is from fear to a focus upon helping others who are dreaming. You move from selfishness to selflessness.

We have hand selected this phrase to lift you up, and encourage you to say this to yourself repeatedly: "I am so blessed." Feel your heart open with gratitude as you say, "I am so blessed, I am so blessed, I am so blessed."

And, yes, it really *is* the truth that you *are* so blessed! How could God create you otherwise? By affirming that you are blessed, you then restructure your very physical core to a more crystalline, high-vibrational energy. The adage "The rich get richer" applies to you, as you magnetically attract more blessings.

Selfishness, Selflessness, and Sacrifice

With all of your blessings upon the love path, you will naturally be guided to share with others. Here is where we need to explain the difference between helping upon the love path and "helping" upon the fear path.

With love-based helping, you are internally guided with an open heart toward giving materially, energetically, or emotionally to others (and that includes animals and the environment as well). You feel even more joyful as you help others to feel joyful. It's about *them*, instead of about "getting them to like you."

Think of yourself as a candle using your flame to light other candles. Your flame isn't diminished as it lights the other wicks. Your light is actually magnified as other candles shine their light, too.

Contrast this with helping actions conducted upon the low-vibrational path of fear. This involves helping others because of guilt, feelings of obligation, or worries that others won't like you or will leave or fire you if you don't help them. In this scenario, you are giving an empty—or even worse, toxic—gift to others. It's the equivalent of handing them a box full of fear energy. There is no love in this form of giving, so the results aren't satisfying or lasting.

What you give, you receive in turn. If you give love, you will receive it. If you give fear, you will receive it. Maybe not from the same person to whom you gave love or fear, but in some way, you always receive the exact mirror energy boomeranged back to you.

Giving upon the low-vibrational fear path is the equivalent of the belief in sacrifice as the ultimate display of love, and a method of appeasement and gaining mercy. There's a superstition that you'll be rewarded for your martyrdom, or that you're a "better person" for having thought of others instead of yourself.

Yet, is suffering and sacrificing truly a "selfless" act of altruism? If the giving is done with strings attached (that is, *I hope to receive appreciation, love, or other rewards*), then it is not at the highest vibration of pure love.

True selflessness does not involve thinking about what you'll receive. The act of giving from love is so joyful and pleasurable that it is its own reward.

Love-based giving is always Divinely guided. This means that you receive an intuitive thought or feeling to help someone in need. Taking action upon this intuition usually results in synchronicities and a sense of having a "magical experience."

This high that you feel as you lovingly give to others is the pipeline connection to Heaven, and the bliss that you seek. As long as you give from love, you will always receive this lasting satisfaction as your reward. There's no need for external awards or recognition.

"Selfishness" is a fear-based path of believing that there isn't enough supply for everyone. It is an out-picturing of the belief in lack. With this belief comes panic and insecurity about having enough. Even if there is enough, the stress of believing there is a lack creates the experience as if there wasn't enough.

The love-based path was demonstrated in the biblical analogy of the loaves and fishes, which was a testament to the multiplication of whatever you joyfully give. Jesus Christ taught and teaches by example as one who is com-pletely upon the path of love.

Selflessness isn't the same as sacrifice, as we've said earlier. Selflessness is the experience of being extremely happy, feeling that you're in the right place and detached from awareness of time, as you give for the joy of giving. This is the path of love.

Within the English language, you can bear witness to the distinctions this way:

- *Self-ish-ness*: The -*ish* refers to identification with the lower self, the egoic belief in a sepa-rate and special self. The focus is upon the self, not others.

- *Self-less-ness*: The -*less* shows a focus upon oneness and the higher self, rather than on the separate lower self.

Selflessness truly is the higher pathway to happiness, health, abundance, and all that you consider desirable and long-lasting. With selflessness, you see that you are one with God and all others. Therefore, you do not harbor judgments about yourself or others. You do not analyze others, and there's never a focus upon dramas.

Like an angel, you see the Divine within yourself and others. This strengthens you beyond any human form of strength. Your knowledge that everyone is a beloved child of God doing the best that they can places you upon the highest road of Heaven that you can experience while still upon the earth. You heal others with your outlook.

Selfishness is the flip side of the idea of sacrifice. With sacrifice, there's a sense of depression and buried anger for others taking advantage of your generosity and not giving you the rewards and respect you deserve. This is the path of fear.

In this same vein, the ego preaches that suffering is the pathway to "salvation," wherein you are forgiven for your detours from Heaven. All of this stems from the ego's mistaken belief that you have departed from God's womb and are now flying solo through the physical universe. A deep-seated guilt arises for having abandoned your Creator and your true home, and guilt always fears reprisal, punishment, and retaliation for your actions.

The entire romantic notion about darkness versus light rests upon these very premises. The ego's imagination creates chaos, instability, and other forms of fear begotten in its own image and likeness.

Selfishness is an outlook of vigilantly protecting yourself from danger. It is uptight, worried, and never at peace—no matter how many accolades or material possessions are accumulated.

Now does this mean that you need to live an ascetic life, denying earthly pleasures in order to reach your nirvana of inner peace? Well, there's certainly a lot to be said for living simply.

For example, we guide you to notice the various stressors you encounter throughout the day, and really analyze their origin. Notice how each stressor appeared in your life. Did you purchase an item because you believed it would bring you prestige, only to find that it is bringing you stress instead? Did you engage in a relationship when you had received internal warning signals to avoid the relationship? Did you neglect an earthly responsibility, and now it has caught up to you?

As you realize how your choices influence your stress levels, you will naturally stop choosing the pathway of stress (which is the same as the pathway of fear).

You don't have to chase after peace, because it was already instilled in you when you were originally created. God, being peace, created you peaceful.

And it's not like a marble statue that you need to chip away at in order to reveal your peaceful self. The parts of yourself that aren't peaceful are illusions of separation and darkness that instantly disappear when the lights of awareness are turned on.

Striving

Accumulating more is the hallmark of the separated ego, which wants to create a substitute for Heaven. Like a "kid in a candy store," the ego continuously strives for a high that is only obtainable through the higher-self consciousness of love and oneness.

Yet the ego is not at all aware of love, just temporary satisfaction. This is where we see humans "chasing the high" that they initially get with that first bite, first sip, or first inhale, or when an item is newly purchased. This high wears off quickly. Then an addictive cycle follows of looking for another way to get that high and keep it.

The ego's highs are necessarily temporary, because God did not create them—fear did.

This is not to say that you can't aspire to have a safe and comfortable home and automobile, the clothing and food that you need, and so forth.

Here is the litmus test to help you recognize if your desires are ego based (with temporary pleasure) or higher-self based (with lasting peace):

- If it's a desire of the ego, the basis is separation, such as trying to impress someone, gain love or approval, get someone to like or forgive you, display how much power or money you have, protect yourself from power plays or attack, win a competition, or feel an addictive high from acquiring the desired object or situation.

- If it's a desire of the higher self, the basis is oneness and love, such as following your inner guidance to further your education for your life purpose, having a place or forum for teaching or healing others, receiving financing to help others, selling your services or goods because they bring blessings to others, or a genuine wish to serve.

With both scenarios, you will receive something in exchange for your efforts. As you can see, the more desirable of the two pathways is love.

You'll also experience an added benefit from following the pathway of love: attracting love-based people who are drawn to your mission, and desire to support and help you. This is contrasted to walking the path of separation and selfishness, which pushes other people away.

The higher-self pathway feels natural and comfortable, like a warm hug. There's no need to sacrifice, please, appease, or appeal for anything to win your peace. You've already got it!

3

Awakening Together

A Message about Your Relationships

Within a relationship, the choices are the same as with your relationship with yourself: the path of fear or love.

Two people may be walking upon the path of fear together, seemingly for the purpose of protecting each other and jointly finding happiness in a fearful world. However, whenever one or more people walk in fear, the experience always results in fear. This is when an inconsistent roller coaster of dramatic emotions ensues within the relationship.

There may be a sense that you'll be happier if you leave this person's side. Yet if you're then walking upon the pathway of fear alone, *you're still on the pathway of fear*, with all of its unpleasant consequences. You may find a new person to walk with upon this path of fear, with the same unsatisfying outcome.

Whether you have a nightmare alone or sleeping next to someone who is also nightmaring, the results are equally terrifying. And yes, when you awaken and the other person holds you comfortingly, there is a temporary relief from fear. The cessation of fear and the feeling of love is the real and true awakening.

The paths of love and fear have no intersections, common grounds, or meeting places. They are entirely different vibrations, like the band of purple on the rainbow running parallel to the band of red. There is no treading in a transitional zone blending the two. You are either on the path of love or on the path of fear.

Just like when you're sleeping, you can be on the pathway of fear and then "awaken" upon the pathway of love. For most humans, there's a jolting roller coaster of bouncing between both pathways. This creates an unsettling sense of instability and confusion.

You cannot be upon both paths simultaneously. Either you are awake to your true reality of living cozily and comfortably within God, or you are asleep to this reality and have forgotten who you are, where you came from, and where you are now.

What you are seeking in your relationships is a merging and sense of oneness, which can only be experienced when two people walk upon the pathway of love together. To do so requires a great deal of awareness and self-honesty, which is why you care enough to learn about these truths.

We shall next explore the detour most often keeping humans asleep and upon the pathway of fear.

The Detour of Boredom

The overriding dream desire of one who is asleep is to awaken from the nightmare of feeling separated from Source God Creator. How to awaken is the process in which there are freewill choices to be made.

The sense of boredom is a restlessness of feeling unhappy with your current scenario. It's like watching television with a remote control perpetually changing the channels. Always seeking the right scene to which you feel entirely connected. Someone or something that entertains, uplifts, and validates you.

This desire for something better would be fine if it were a love-based intention to help others or to supply yourself with the means to meet your needs. The trouble with boredom is that it presents endless mountains to climb. When you reach the peak of one, you see a thousand more before you. This elicits a deep-seated feeling of futility and a *What's the use?* jaded approach to life.

These are the underlying processes, usually unconscious, behind the existential drive to find meaning. When humans strive to answer the questions *Why am I here?* and *What is my purpose?* they are really expressing dissatisfaction with their true spiritual state of being a beloved child of God, resting within God's mind and heart.

Restlessness and boredom are desires for something to fill the emptiness and bring peace, happiness, and a sense of meaning. There's a frantic reach for something or somebody, such as some "magical" food, substance, activity, or relationship, to fill the spaces and lead to wholeness—anything to temporarily dull the sense of painful separation. It is the futile search for the "key" to happiness.

When you feel hungry for something to make you "feel better," this is a sure sign of being upon the pathway of fear. With true physical or emotional hunger arising from normal human needs, there is a smoothly Divine process of creating and attracting fulfillment. This differs sharply from the broad shotgun approach to finding whatever will momentarily satiate you.

In relationships, this process is demonstrated as a coming together to mutually seek out the key. The unconscious agreement is for each person to entertain the other to assuage boredom. Yet, how is this possible when neither person lacks for meaning or excitement in spiritual truth?

Please contemplate this truth: You and every person you have ever met and will ever meet are the same out-picturing of God's complete and pure love. Every physical, emotional, and mental need is instantly fulfilled. So, in spiritual truth, boredom and restlessness are impossible.

The search for the next greatest thing or person is the same drive invoking the dream of fear and the ego in the first place, like a perpetually looping movie with the same plot. The ego's sense of reality is based upon insatiable desire for its own definition of perfection. The ego rejects God's gifts of Divine perfection, in favor of a do-it-yourself, laborious approach to perfection.

Relationships are often the ego's way of alleviating boredom, and looking for an avenue to fulfill its endless needs for validation and gratification. These fearful pathways of togetherness are what you would term "toxic" or "dysfunctional" relationships. They begin in a quest that cannot be fulfilled (to find Heaven externally) and end with an equally unfulfilling crescendo of drama, suffering, and misery.

When a relationship begins with an empty premise of "Please save me from this separation condition of loneliness, boredom, danger, or other form of lack," then it forms upon the bumpy and rocky pathway of fear.

Yet, please do not misunderstand our overview of relationships, as true partnerships can be an avenue by which you rediscover God and Heaven within.

The Search for Validation

If all you've "known" in your physical life is guilt and feelings of unworthiness, then you were born and raised upon the pathway of fear. You literally have amnesia about your Divine origin and are living within the nightmarish "reality" of competing to get your needs met.

Yet within every person who treads upon the pathway of fear, there's a beckoning melody in the far reaches of their soul, calling them to return to their Heavenly home. Some mistake this as a desire for death, believing that peace is only possible once the physical body ceases to function. Yet, for the person whose consciousness is focused upon fear, even physical death does not bring relief.

"Validation" is the unconscious desire to be reminded of who you really are. It is expressed in the physical world as desires for approval, rewards, promotions, applause, and other benchmarks that give you a sense of being better than—or at least as good as—other people.

Within relationships, the desire for validation is expressed as exchanging compliments with one another. The ultimate "reward" within a relationship is the verbal and physical expression of mutual love, often accompanied by a ceremony to celebrate this love publicly.

Yet, if two people can mirror *true* love to one another, then they awaken together to their Divine reality of being one in God's love. They remember that they are really back home in Heaven together within God's embrace. This is the genuine and lasting reward, and the real purpose of relationships.

Those who take actions to remember God's love are most likely to awaken themselves to their true reality and true love. When two or more people jointly focus upon remembering their true spiritual identities, they can help awaken one another to the reality of true love.

Many relationships waver between glimpses of true love and the "love" espoused by the pathway of fear. Like a casino slot machine that occasionally pays out a large sum, the relationship holds the promise of a return to that pure love, which is attempted through various means—some fear based and some love based.

For example, if someone criticizes you, that's the ego doing the judging, because only the ego judges. That means the other person isn't happy. No one centered on the ego's perceptions is happy. Have compassion for them, and don't judge them in return for being judgmental or you will be unhappy, too.

Relationships give you the opportunity to find God, or experience the opposite pole of cold and lonely separation. We are handing you a healing pair of glasses, so that you can see the dazzling brightness of Godliness within everyone you meet, including within yourself. This light is so bright that it obliterates any awareness of separated human bodies. Instead of seeing bodily outlines, you see the magnificent glow of God's life force shining back at you. This is the form of mirroring that brings validation for your true self and the experience of lasting satisfaction.

A relationship feels best when it is selfless, and one partner is not viewed as the vehicle through which the other attains satisfaction. In a selfless relationship, the focus is upon each person being wholly aware of the fullness of God's love and then walking next to each other upon this pathway of love. Perhaps the two partners consciously form a team to help others awaken to their divinity, as well.

A "God team" of people who are awake to their true identity are literally angels in the physical world. Picture a room full of children sleeping upon cots, each shaking from the nightmares they are experiencing. Then imagine a few of the children waking up and realizing that the nightmares weren't real, and then taking the time to gently awaken the other children. This is your role and your purpose within love-based relationships.

How you awaken others is the next matter of discourse.

4

Spiritual Perfection

A Message about Forgiveness

Judgment is a mental habit, designed to push away uncomfortable feelings. It's easier to label someone as "bad" or "good" than to process the variety of emotions triggered by their behaviors. The tangled yarn of mixed emotions beneath judgment can include forms of fear such as shock, grief, guilt, betrayal, disappointment, and insecurity.

Someone's egoic behavior may also trigger memories of your past experiences around which you still harbor emotional pain. In this case, your judgment would be a wall that you erect to prevent additional pain.

The physical truth is that human egos are based upon a fear ideology, and therefore to the ego, every decision and action is worthy of being judged. Fearful behavior stems from fearful beliefs.

The ego prides itself on being separated from others in a uniquely special and better way. To maintain this illusion, it's necessary for the ego to target other people's egos.

To see similarity or hold compassion is threatening to the ego's fortification mission. The ego has built strong fortress walls of judgment to protect it from noticing that other people's egos are identical to itself.

Those who are spiritual students do understand the high price they pay for judging. For the most part, they choose compassion instead of judgment. For this choice, they are rewarded with greater inner peace.

Yet, even the most devout spiritual students seem to have their limits with respect to who they can compassionately forgive. For everyone, the standards are different.

However, most humans would say that someone who inflicts grievous pain is not worthy of being "rewarded" with forgiveness. "An eye for an eye" to them means retaliation, and that they should suffer in exchange for the suffering they brought to others.

In this philosophy, forgiving is akin to saying, "What you did was okay." In truth, forgiveness is not the same as passivity or pardoning.

Yet, as we will continue to discuss with you, there are four levels of forgiveness:

- *Faux forgiving*, where you say that you forgive someone, without really meaning it.

- *Forgiving from judgment*, where you forgive someone so that you can be the "better person," but really you are still harboring resentment.

- *Forgiving from the heart*, where you have compassion for the person, knowing that they made a mistake.

- *Forgiving from spiritual truth*, which says that errors are illusions and actually did not occur. Therefore, no judgment is possible, and forgiveness makes no sense because there's nothing to forgive.

Judging seems to be its own reward, as it helps you to distance yourself from those whose actions are distasteful to you. If you've been hurt by another person, you want to avoid being hurt again.

In the physical world, as we've been discussing, people can either walk the pathway of love or fear at each moment. You cannot walk upon both pathways simultaneously.

Those whom you would consider to be "trustworthy" or "good" people spend most of their time upon the love pathway. Then something happens to trigger their egoic fears, and they jump to the fear pathway.

Actions always follow the pathway you're on, so:

- If you're on the love pathway, your actions will be selfless and entail thoughtfulness, compassion, gentleness, and other aspects of love.

- If you're on the fear pathway, your actions will be selfish and exhibit thoughtlessness, competitiveness, harshness, and other aspects of fear.

Vacillating between the love and fear pathways creates confusion in relationships. You thought you knew this person who was largely on the love pathway, and then they changed. What happened? The ego argues that you never knew this person at all—that they were a fake and phony, and you can't trust them.

Yet, every human has an emotional trigger propelling them into fear-based thoughts and actions. If you judge every person for acting fearfully, you will be alone. You will also harshly judge yourself for acting fearfully. There are no 100 percent love-based people on the planet, including yourself.

Judgment creates loneliness as you cast away those who may trigger pain. You work hard to stay safe, even at the cost of being alone. You huddle within your fortress of judgment, where dragons and moats keep everyone far away. In turn, other people judge you as cold, distant, aloof, and so forth.

The high price of judgment includes isolation from yourself as well. You don't recognize yourself as a judgmental person, *because that's not the true you!* Your true self is entirely loving, and you can feel this positive resonance within yourself each time you choose a loving thought or action. If you choose fear-based outlooks and actions, you can feel a physically palpable discomfort.

The adage "As you judge others, so you judge yourself" applies here, because there is no true separation between you and others.

This may help you to fully understand this important message: Think of a figure 8 with its continuous loop. One loop on the 8 is you, and the other loop is someone else. Notice how the two loops are perpetually connected and perfect mirrors of each other.

What you think of another person is cast forward to the adjoining loop as an energy traveling around the figure 8, affecting both of you. The egoic fear energy feels sharp, cold, and lonely, and both sides of the figure 8 are cast into a restrictive darkness together.

Contrast this with sending loving energy to the other loop of the figure 8, and *this* energy traveling back to you.

It feels like a warm, gentle hug that envelops and supports you both. This is an expansive energy that shines brightly like God's love, or the physical rays of the sun.

Opinions about others always loop back to you. For example, if someone judges you, beware of the mental reaction of automatically judging them in return for being a "judgmental person." Judging someone for being in their ego casts you into your ego as well.

A similar loop occurs when you "catch" yourself being judgmental, and then you harshly judge yourself for walking upon the path of fear. The ego insists upon human perfectionism as a way of feeling better than others.

Any form of judgment is an affirmation that you are separate from other people. It denies the spiritual truth of the figure-8 loop connecting and affecting you.

Since separation is the most nightmarish illusion, judgment comes at the high price of eliciting deep emotional pain due to feeling lonely, abandoned, isolated, and misunderstood. The ego argues that judgment is justified because the other person's actions were unforgivable.

Discernment Instead of Judgment

When you think of everyone upon the planet, here's another analogy to illustrate your Divine connection:

Think of a large, healthy tree with billions of leaves. Each leaf represents a person. While the leaves appear to be separated, they are actually all connected to the same tree, representing God.

Each leaf may seem to be having its own experience. Perhaps the wind or rain hits some leaves more than others, and maybe some receive more sunshine than others. Yet, each leaf is part of the greater whole comprising a tree. So it is with you and everyone on this planet. What you do affects others, and vice versa. You truly are kin with everyone.

Remember that we are speaking of spiritual truths and nonduality, which only sees and acknowledges love. This involves seeing others as God sees everyone: as beloved children who are purposefully created with love.

Just like some children, some adults may act in ways that seem thoughtless and hurtful. Certain behavior seems calculated without regard for others' feelings or safety. In other words, some people spend most—or all—of their lives walking upon the path of fear.

This is the definition of selfish behavior, because the ego sees itself as its own universe. Remember that the ego is always jockeying to feel above, or better than, others, so it judges and compares to achieve this end. To the ego, other people are objects to use for its own needs, or competitors for a mutually desirable objective. The ego also views love as weakness, and anger as strength.

The ego is miserable and lonely, and always searching for something external to squelch its misery.

Think of a television remote control, please. In the physical world of duality, there are two channels on this remote control: *love* or *fear*. You can think and act either from love or from fear. There are no in-between channels. It truly is a choice between happiness and misery.

When you judge yourself or someone else, you are automatically cast onto the path of fear and misery—even if the judgment seems justified. That's where discernment comes in to save the day.

Consider these key differences between judgment and discernment:

Judgment	Discernment
Labels something (or someone) as "good" or "bad"	Says "I'm attracted to this [or them]," or "I'm not attracted to this [or them]"
Denies feelings and has no compassion	Acknowledges feelings, including whether or not you're attracted to this
Is one-dimensional and only sees faults	Sees the various levels involved

Let's take an example of you not liking the smell of cigarette smoke. If someone smokes a cigarette near you, you can react from judgment (fear) or discernment (love):

- Judgment, fear, and the ego would label the cigarette and the smoker "bad" or use even harsher words.

- Discernment, love, and the true self would say, "I'm not attracted to the smell or the energy of cigarette smoke or those who smell like cigarettes. I will stay away."

With discernment, there's no labeling of the other person. There's an acknowledgment of your honest feelings.

Discernment is the expression of being on the love pathway. If you are upon the pathway of love, you will be attracted to the energy of love. You will not be attracted by the energy of fear. Those who live primarily upon the pathway of love may not even encounter or notice the energy of fear. Remember that the pathways of love and fear have no intersections or common ground, but you can bounce back and forth between the two pathways.

Holding loving thoughts does lead to being universally compassionate toward yourself and everyone. It softens you in a strong way.

However, being loving does not mean that you need to spend time with those who are walking the pathway of fear. You can, however, *inspire* through your living example of the peace and joy of walking upon the pathway of love.

You can also inspire social and global change through your willingness to be a positive example. Love is honest, and that includes you *speaking from* your heart about matters that *speak to* your heart.

For those people whom you deeply care about, and perhaps are worried about, we do hear your prayers to alleviate their suffering. We do intervene to the degree that each person chooses to allow our support.

Those who walk upon the pathway of fear consider themselves "tough" and "strong," and their egos are threatened by anything soft, such as emotions like happiness, and even health. So they push these gifts away.

Compassion reveals that those who are afraid have had life experiences that have taught them this path. Many do not know anything but the fear that the world is a dangerous and competitive place. This is what they experience, as a result of this belief . . . which many times was passed along by their elders.

Someone who is unaware of any pathway except for fear is ignorant of other options. For them, life is a series of major disappointments interspersed with minor moments of joy. They pray for help, yet refuse to listen to the guidance we offer up like a life raft.

The Double Error of Guilt

Similar to judgment, guilt is a fear-based focus upon mistakes or errors. We watch humans harboring guilt about what they did or didn't do. In this sense, guilt *is* judgment cast upon yourself.

Guilt is a double-edged error, because it begins with the faulty premise that you have done anything that could undo God's handiwork of Divine spiritual perfection. Any pain that you inflict upon others is part of the illusory world of fear. This does not excuse or justify fear-based actions that are considered cruel or thoughtless. It simply means that all of the pain, lack, and suffering is within the nightmarish illusion, not in any lasting reality.

From where we are, we watch how guilt weighs down the human heart, binding it with such heaviness that love seems like a faraway fantasy. Guilt leads to feelings of unworthiness, including feeling unworthy of accepting God's unconditional love, help, and Divine guidance.

Those who feel guilty are also afraid of punishment. In fact, there's an unconscious belief that if you're punished, then the "crime" that you enacted will be forgiven. To punish yourself for your perceived crimes, you may deny yourself happiness or walk right into a situation that will result in pain, perceived as "punishment" or "karma."

This double-edged error of believing that you're guilty and then judging yourself for it creates distractions from your Heavenly calling—what you term your "life purpose."

Your prayers for our intervention are effective, of course, in relieving you from the burden of guilt. And even more effective is the curative power of unconditional love.

God only knows, sees, and feels love. God acknowledges your true self, as originally created: innocent, guiltless, and loving. This is unconditional love, which you can tap into directly by saying the name of God repeatedly. The name of God attunes you to the memory of your current residence within the womb of Divine unconditional love.

As you remember this primary spiritual truth, you feel your heart warm and open to love. Your heart is a portal through which God's love travels to others in need.

When enough people walk upon the pathway of love, the collective uplifting energy calls to those who are upon the pathway of fear. Like a magnet pulling them upward, they feel a familiar sense they faintly recall from their Heavenly life. The sense of being unconditionally loved is the most basic memory and driving force within each sentient being—human, animal, bird, or fish.

Everyone remembers pure love, because everyone still lives within that pure love of God. Some futilely struggle to find that feeling with externals. This never works.

Those who *do* find Heaven during their earthly life are those who exude unconditional love. Instead of waiting to be unconditionally loved by others, they send the unconditional love from their mind and heart . . . including toward themselves.

Unconditional love lifts you up, and insulates you from others' egoic energies and actions. The Divine light of God glows within, from, and around you. You love yourself at the same level as you love everyone else, because you love God's creations.

There's no sense that you're less or better than anyone else, because that would be a belief in separation that is the foundation of the pathway of fear. You respect yourself and others. You naturally attract and meet others who are also unconditionally loving, so you enjoy healthy relationships.

Sometimes spirituality is misunderstood as a call to be saintlike and perfect. Again, only the ego is concerned with outward appearances of perfection. The ego judges, so it naturally fears being judged itself.

The path of love acknowledges that people aren't humanly perfect, but that they are spiritually perfect. You are a role model of Divine spiritual perfection, by your decision to focus upon unconditional love rather than judgmental fear.

5

Your Four Bodies

A Message about Healing

When you fully awaken to the realization of your divinity and true identity and home, there's no more chasing, no competing, no forcing, and no controlling to meet your human needs. Everything that you need is automatically met by flow and attraction, similar to a dream.

All physical bodies, whether human, animal, fish, bird, or plant, need physical nourishment and appropriate shelter. The body is a result of the ego's desire to have an experience apart from God, and it functions as a housing to seemingly contain and carry your soul. The body can be used in service of either love or fear while in the dream.

We would like to explain in further detail the origination and function of your body, so that you can maintain and utilize it at optimum high-vibrational levels.

The Origin of the Ego

As we've discussed, God's love energy is endless and everywhere, and so is the substance of the endless universe. Right at this moment, you are safely snuggled into the warm folds and embrace of God's eternal love. Like a newborn baby cradled by a parent, you feel completely loved, appreciated, needed, and respected. You have no needs, no fears, no worries, and no anxieties. You feel complete and whole.

So the real and true you does not have a physical body. You are a bright light soul, a spark of divinity, merged with others who are on the same wavelength as you. Everyone and everything is your soul mate.

Somewhere along the line, like a short in an electrical circuit, you and your soul mates had a shared nightmare about being in a faraway land, apart from one another. This nightmare is terrifying. Like a lost child seeking its parent, everyone sharing this collective nightmare is equally upset, insecure, and frightened.

In this physical dream of separation, you have four bodies in layers:

- *The physical body*: The dense outer-shell housing for your experience as a separated being, this body functions as an outline distinguishing where you end and other people begin. The physical body can also be used within the nightmare as a way of awakening others who are asleep to oneness.

- *The emotional body*: Sometimes referred to as your "inner child," your emotional body is pure feelings and sensitivity. Its primal drive is to reconnect with that Heavenly feeling of being completely loved, safe, and accepted. The emotional body craves merging with another person, just as it remembers being merged with all others and God.

- *The intellectual body*: This is the creator within you, which is governed by either selfishness (ego) or selflessness (true self). God endowed you with every spiritual gift, including the ability to think creations into form. When you create from fear, the results are unsatisfying and short-lived. When you create from selfless love, the results reflect God and so are fulfilling and eternal.

- *The energetic or light body*: Sometimes called your "aura," this body registers your energy levels (for example, *excited*, *tired*, *relaxed*, or *peaceful*). Your light body also radiates the effects of love energy to the physical, emotional, and intellectual bodies. It is the engine of the self-regulating system of the four bodies, with an autocorrection that keeps all of them healthy and balanced.

  In addition, the energy body is the way-station womb of your creations. Once you decide or focus on something, the thought is the seed that then grows within the garden of your energy body. Those who are sensitive to energy can feel or see what you think about by connecting with your energy body. Once your thoughts have germinated, they then form their own physical bodies.

Energy Density

As you've seen and felt, energy waves vibrate at differing rates. We use the rainbow analogy to explain that the path of fear is akin to the band of red upon the rainbow, with slow vibrations. And the path of love is analogous to the violet band of light, with the highest vibrations. While these two color bands are upon the same spectrum, they never connect or intersect. They do blend by the vibrations of interim colors of orange, yellow, green, and blue.

The red color represents the densest physical energy, and the ego. This is why red is symbolic of the devil, hell, "stop," and physical lust. The slowest vibrations also emit a low and unharmonious sound that all beings can hear on a subconscious, visceral level.

The purple color is symbolic of spirituality, royalty, abundance, and fearlessness about expressing your authentic self. The highest of the vibrations upon the physical plane, purple emits harmonious symphonies of celestial music. So you may think of the love path as being immersed in this highest vibration.

Healing and Harmonizing the Body

Physical bodies and other objects are composed of energy vibrating slowly enough to achieve density. You can harmonize your physical body by returning to a oneness consciousness with your other bodies. This involves uniting your emotions, intellect, and energy with your physical body.

Illness and accidents are the effects of rejecting or judging one or more of your four bodies. You'll recall from our previous discussion that judging is always upon the pathway of fear, while discernment is of love. With judging, there's a label of "good" or "bad," while with discernment, there are honest reactions of attraction or repelling.

As an example, if you are feeling lonely—which every person does while believing in the illusion of separation—you can either *love* this feeling or judge it as embarrassing or unacceptable.

"Loving loneliness" does not mean that you're welcoming this emotion to take up permanent residence within your life. Loving an emotion means that you're acknowledging it and nurturing it like a caring parent holding a crying infant. The parent, not wanting the infant to continue crying, will comfort the baby until it is calm.

When you comfort your emotions, you are accepting yourself as God unconditionally accepts you. Your emotional body is the child within you who is natural, honest, and expressive. Your emotional child wants to be listened to.

If you reject your feelings as being unacceptable, you are rejecting your child within. This results in increased emotions of sadness, anger, and anxiety.

Your feelings are a feedback system helping you to monitor which pathway (love or fear) you are walking upon. If you feel "negative" emotions, you know you're on the fear path. Judging negative emotions only compounds and increases them.

If you feel ashamed of your feelings, it's the same as being ashamed of who you are. This creates further separation within the dream of separation. You distance yourself *from* yourself, as someone would a person they are ashamed to be seen with.

Similarly, rejecting your thoughts as unacceptable causes a dissociation effect, where you feel as if you're floating above your body in a surreal dreamlike movie.

We have witnessed humans attempt to force themselves to hold positive thoughts, thereby burying the "negative" thoughts crying for attention.

A splintering effect also occurs if you deem that your energy levels are unacceptably high or low. The ego is a harsh judge who refuses to hear reason from the physical, emotional, intellectual, or energy bodies—even though these bodies have important messages to deliver.

The key to health is to accept, love, and have compassion for all of your four earthly bodies. No one likes to be judged or rejected, and that includes *you*. You can literally love yourself to complete health by having a compassionate parental relationship with yourself. This means that you care deeply for, guide, and manage yourself.

For instance, continuing with the example of loneliness, at first you may not be aware of what the feeling is or where it originated. So you begin with the feelings you can identify, such as pangs of emptiness, undeservingness, fears that others don't enjoy your company, and so forth.

These are admittedly not enjoyable feelings to entertain. It can feel easier to reject or numb them. There's a sense of feeling worse about yourself if you own up to "less than perfect" feelings.

This slippery-slope process then affects the intellectual, energy, and physical bodies. A person who rejects the emotional symptoms of loneliness may then have thoughts of being unworthy, which in turn lowers the person's energy levels, which then impacts their physical health.

This is the domino effect of judging yourself. Rejecting any part of your physical, emotional, intellectual, or energetic self always results in the opposite of Heaven. Instead of nestling deeply into the comfortable folds of God's love, you withdraw into the folds of cold darkness, which compounds the sense of separation, loneliness, and feeling unloved.

The path of healing is the same as the path of love: unconditional compassion and acceptance for that which seems unacceptable to the perfectionistic, judgmental ego.

The reason why medicine and other curative programs are effective in healing is that the patient trusts the healer. The patient relaxes, like an infant in a caring parent's arms, viewing the healer as the Source. Fear and judgment are eradicated, and the patient is healed.

God's love is everywhere, including within the nightmare of separation and within every cell of your physical body. Your dream decisions determine what occurs next for you and your body.

How Your Bodies Affect Relationships

Your four bodies are your cooperative teammates during the dream of separation. They're messengers bringing you feedback about your experience. If you reject their messages because you dislike anything "negative," it's similar to a military officer not listening to soldiers reporting an imminent invasion.

We angels will lend you our strength to listen to less-than-pleasant news from your bodies. Most of the time, they complain about unacceptable situations compromising their balance and health *that need attention and addressing.*

For example, your emotional body has needs that involve merging with others to recharge itself with the pure love it remembers from Heaven. The emotional body seeks someone synchronized with its own vibration as a way of mirroring or validating its own worth. This process is where the adage "Like attracts like" originates.

When you first meet a person with such a matching vibration, the emotional body feels something similar to the oneness of merging in Heaven. It feels validated to find its twin, and loneliness and feelings of separation are alleviated.

If both people are on the path of love together, this partnership will be joyful and harmonious. Yet, that wish is often unrealistic because of the tendency for one partner to jump to the fear pathway.

When you are on a different pathway from your partner, you will feel lonely and abandoned. The other person's *physical body* is there with you, but their *emotional body* is elsewhere. You literally are on two different wavelengths.

So your emotional body will tell you that it hurts and doesn't feel loved, and ask you as its parent to please take action to alleviate these painful feelings.

This is where your *intellectual body* has the freewill power to choose what to do next, such as:

- Ignore the feelings
- Blame the partner or yourself
- Numb the feelings with an addictive behavior or substance

These are examples of reconnecting with your partner by lowering your own vibrations to meet them upon the pathway of fear. We angels do this for our patron humans all the time, without harm. However, humans are prone to amnesia about unconditional love, so they become trapped within the illusion of fear.

The intellectual body upon the path of love would make choices like these:

- Feeling compassion (not pity) for the partner
- Forgiving the partner and yourself
- Having an honest discussion and lovingly sharing with the partner
- Loving the partner and yourself
- Acknowledging your oneness without guilt or blame

Health and Lifestyle

The main reason why you sense us angels guiding your lifestyle choices about food, drink, exercise, and sleep is because we are helping you to regulate each body at its optimum levels. You really don't need anything for your true self, as all of your needs are equally and continuously met. In the dream of separation, though, your bodies require attention.

Just as your relationships with others are determined by the pathway choice of fear or love, so is your relationship with your physical, emotional, intellectual, and energetic bodies. Each of your four bodies is equally important to functioning as a whole team. Your four bodies each have a life force, intelligence, and ego of their own.

In the physical world, *every being*—including the physical, emotional, intellectual, and energetic bodies—*is seeking the Heavenly sense of belonging, love, and union.* Once you understand this important and basic principle, you will know how to feed and balance your bodies for optimal functioning.

You are seeking the sense of belonging, love, and union you remember from Heaven. In the physical dream, each of your four bodies also craves belonging, love, and union.

Your consciousness is the "I" who manages your body. Your true-self consciousness already feels loved, so your true self is not seeking or craving love. However, in the separated consciousness of the ego, there is a lack of love. So the ego continually looks outwardly for the sense of belonging, love, and union.

What this means in practical terms is that your "I" (your consciousness) can heal and balance you within the physical dream by helping your four bodies feel like they belong, are loved, and are one with each other.

Instead of rejecting or judging any part of yourself, have compassion, like a counselor working with a client. This isn't the same as passively accepting destructive habits. In fact, those habits are developed in a misguided attempt to feel love in external ways. Be an unconditionally loving coach to yourself, and you'll feel loved and accepted . . . and won't look for these conditions externally.

— **Your physical body craves loving touch.** Be sure to nurture yourself with loving self-embraces, hugs from someone who is on the love pathway, the touch of a caring bodyworker, or cuddles from an animal companion. *Give yourself physical nurturing.*

— **Your emotional body needs to feel safe, loved, and listened to.** You can nurture your emotional body by listening to your feelings, especially the uncomfortable emotions. Your four bodies always speak their truth to you, and your consciousness may feel intimidated when the emotions ask you to make changes. For example, if your emotional body is unhappy in a career or relationship, you will hear the message to either heal or leave the unhappy situation. You don't need to rule your life by your emotions or act upon every feeling you have—but you do need to listen to them. *Give yourself emotional understanding.*

— **Your intellectual body requires quiet so that it can process and understand Divine messages.** One of the reasons why you may feel disconnected from God is that your mind or environment is too noisy to hear the constant subtle messages. *Give yourself quiet time daily.*

— **Your energetic body matches the energy of what it comes into contact with.** So, it is influenced by the music and radio shows you listen to, the programs you watch, your conversations, the people with whom you interact, where you work, and so forth. Your energetic body will function smoothly at a high vibration when it interacts with other high vibrations.

Eating foods with high energy, such as freshly picked, organic sun-ripened produce, will keep your energy high. If you want to know if a food has high life-force energy, hold the food and silently ask it if it loves you. High-vibrational food exudes love and will tell you so.

Examples of low vibrations include fear-based music or television programs; gatherings of people in competitive situations solidifying separation beliefs; and many chemicals, including pesticides, which are designed to kill.

Artificially "boosting" your energy through the use of stimulant chemicals actually has the reverse effect. Your energetic body needs recharging periods, so resting when tired is the equivalent of listening to your emotions when upset. Rest when you need to, and you'll harmonize. *Give yourself high-vibrational foods, surround yourself with positivity, and balance yourself with rest.*

Harmonizing Is Healing

Healing should rightly be termed "revealing," because it is the process of revealing your perfectly healthy self through harmonizing each of your four bodies together.

If something strikes you as uncomfortable, painful, repellent, and so on, pay attention to these signals. *Instead of trying to find some person, object, or situation to help you feel loved, be a loving parent to yourself:*

- Listen to your physical body's complaints and directly inquire what it needs from you.

- Listen to your emotional body's feelings and ask what they mean and what they need from you.

- Listen to your intellectual body's ideas, insights, and epiphanies, and you will have a trustworthy road map that will provide for you and keep you safe.

- Listen to your energetic body's energy fluctuations. Rest when you're tired, and adjust your diet and surroundings if your energy doesn't rebound after a period of rest.

By nurturing your bodies, you'll be satiated and won't need externals to fill you up. You'll experience the Heavenly sense of belonging, love, and union within yourself. The physical dream of separation then becomes an enjoyable, happy dream, filled with synchronicity and pleasant experiences.

Listening to yourself with unconditional love harmonizes your health, which is the basis of true healing.

6

The Gift of Surrender

A Message about Letting Go

The entire reason for the dream of separation was a desire to experience autonomy and free will. It's impossible to be apart from your Creator, except in a dream such as you're experiencing now. Granted, the dream is extremely realistic, ongoing, and suffused with strong emotions.

You were given the complete spiritual power of creation, because you were made in the image and likeness of the Creator. So when you were given carte blanche ability to create whatever you desired, this included trying the dream of separation.

As we've discussed, anything that you create from love is fulfilling and lasting, while anything created from a fearful motivation (that is, insecurity, guilt, anger, revenge, competition, and so forth) is unsatisfying and short-lived.

The ego sees itself in competition with God to be the Supreme Creator. It stubbornly insists that fear keeps it safe, because defensiveness and vigilance can foresee and forestall dangers. The ego takes pride in the situations it creates, even though those situations are what you would call "disasters" and "drama." The ego is like the person who pinches a baby to elicit its cries in order to then be able to heroically comfort the crying baby.

Just as the ingredients you put into the batter determine the taste and appearance of the cake, so too does your input of a fearful or loving motivation determine your outcome. If you prefer your life fulfilling and stable, then choose loving motivations (that is, selflessness, caring, compassion, joyfulness, and the like).

And while generously giving to others *is* a loving act, we angels will help ensure that your motivations for generosity truly are loving. We do witness some humans *acting* generously because of fearful motivations, such as guilt, fear of conflict, or trying to curry the other person's favor.

Giving as you are joyfully guided ensures that you are in alignment with love. So, you will also receive since you are one with all to whom you give.

Attaining and Blaming: Why Problems Arise

Your true spiritual home, which you remember either consciously or unconsciously, is purely harmonious. How could Heaven be otherwise, since there are no unfulfilled needs and no competition?

So even in this dream of living in separated physical bodies, you can feel what it's like to live without problems, worries, or concerns.

You crave peace within your physical, emotional, intellectual, and energetic bodies. The question is how to achieve Heavenly peace within the dream of separation? Until a true understanding occurs, humans attempt to achieve peace through external means.

Logically, it makes no sense to try to find *inner* peace in *outer* ways. Yet, the dream of separation is founded upon seeking that which you believe you don't have. A fulfilled soul can only be unfulfilled in an illusion.

There are two main categories of actions that lead to the experience of human problems: attaining and blaming. Both of these actions are attempts to find the same level of pure unconditional love everyone remembers experiencing in Heaven:

— **Attaining.** This involves trying to buy, possess, own, or earn something that gains outward approval from others. For example, purchasing a fancy automobile or seeking an award because you want others to be impressed.

Approval for what you *own* or *do* is a synthetic version of the total love that you feel in Heaven, where you are universally approved of for who you *are*—since God created everyone's soul with equally magnificent depths and gifts. In Heaven, you feel the kinship of all souls, who are merged within God's loving embrace.

Chasing after a possession or condition to gain unconditional love is an endlessly futile pursuit. Even if you were to gain worldwide approval (which no human has ever done, by the way), it would not come close to the delicious sense of belonging that you have in Heaven.

Happily, you can have this same sense of belonging within the dream of separation—in plain language: you can be happy here upon Earth. We will continue to guide you in this direction through our messages within these pages and those given to you directly through your feelings, knowingness, visions, and spiritual sense of hearing.

— **Blaming.** This involves deflecting and explaining unhappiness by blaming someone or something else. Instead of looking within for solutions, the human ego casts the blame upon others: "It's the government's fault," "It's my parents' fault," "It's my spouse's fault," and so forth.

Seeking external reasons for unhappiness is just as futile as seeking external conditions for happiness. The only reason for unhappiness is because of feeling detached from the umbilical cord of God's nurturing love. Yet, it's impossible to be detached from God, except for in the nightmarish dream of separation. The only way out is to awaken from the dream.

Omnipresent God

God is your Creator and the Source of the love that fulfills you. God bestowed all spiritual gifts upon you when you were created. These gifts are with you in the dream of separation. You did not run away from your Heavenly home and forget to take your valuable spiritual gifts. They are part of your true identity.

Although it feels like a realistic dream, with separated people who are each competing to have their needs met, the truth is that you, and everyone, have the spiritual gifts to resolve any problems arising within the dream.

God creates by shining love, like the sun sharing warm light rays. There is no sense of lack or fear of running out of a limited supply of love or light—because God *is* everything and God *is* love. God's presence and love are everywhere, including within you, every person, and every situation.

In exactly the same way, you create with every loving action, feeling, thought, or energy. And in the physical dream of separation, you can also create with fearful actions, feelings, thoughts, or energy—albeit without the satisfying or lasting results of creating from love.

God is wisdom, and your mind is one with the infinite wisdom of God's Divine mind. Therefore, you have access to all solutions to any apparent problems. As we've discussed, seeking anything—including answers—externally is a futile chase.

God made you a self-contained universe, in which the means to fulfill all of your needs are continuously supplied. Yet, the only way to experience this fulfillment and peace is by knowing that you already have them. Any attempt to look for fulfillment and peace outside of yourself is a waste of time and energy, and a block to actually finding it *within* yourself.

God is within you and you are within God. No situation or part of you is away from God, since God is everywhere.

In the separated dream, it can appear that God is far away, and too busy to answer your prayers. Because you are a creator, you can create from this premise . . . and the results will be unsatisfying, short-lived, and probably terrifying and painful.

When a problem arises, there are three ways to deal with it:

1. Attaining: Trying to fix the issue by gaining something external, such as buying or winning something. These attempts always lead to short-term bursts of pleasure, which can be confused with satisfaction and happiness.

2. Blaming: Pointing fingers at people, organizations, or conditions that "prevent" you from attaining the object or condition you believe will give you happiness. The ego believes if you can eliminate or change the person who is to blame, then happiness will follow. The ego will argue that there is a villain causing the unhappiness, yet blaming a "villain" will not lead to your happiness.

Related to blaming is the process of putting external conditions upon happiness, such as "I could be happy if the world was at peace." And blaming oneself for unhappiness is identical to blaming others, because blame is always a separation thought of someone being "bad." Blame never seeks for solutions, nor does it ever find solutions except for punishment and revenge . . . both of which do not lead to happiness for the blamer.

3. Creating: This involves these two steps:

- *Knowing* that God is within you, within everyone, and within every situation. If you need to increase your faith, prayer can restore your innate spiritual knowledge. Faith is believing, while knowledge is knowing.

- *Revealing* God within you, within everyone, and within every situation. Remember that "healing" is more correctly termed "revealing" the spiritual truth that God—being peace, health, abundance, and all that's considered goodness—is within you, within everyone, and within every situation. One way is to "call" to God, such as *I call upon God to reveal the love* [or health, wisdom, abundance, or whatever else seems to be "lacking"] *that is inherently within* [name of person or situation]." By peeling back the superficial illusion of problems, you will always find God's solutions ready to undo the fear-based creations.

God gave you the spiritual power to create, and you have internal signals within your physical, emotional, intellectual, and energetic bodies to instantly and accurately let you know if you're creating from love or from fear.

If you're creating from love, you'll feel that familiar Heavenly warmth, safety, unconditional love, and comfort. Even more, your happiness shines with God's glowing love, which other people recognize at a visceral level and are attracted to. Creating from love is analogous to "The rich get richer," because happiness creates further happiness.

If you're creating from fear, you'll feel alone, abandoned, cold, and afraid. As we've discussed, trying to "cure" these feelings through external means of attaining or blaming only leads you further away from true and lasting happiness. So, blaming someone or something else for your unhappiness can never solve problems, nor can attaining an object or accomplishments.

The Gift of Surrender

Your mind and God's mind are completely and forever joined. It's the equivalent of you having full access to the universe's greatest computer and wisest advisor! Everything that is God's is also yours.

You may think of the merging of your mind with God's mind as your "upper mind." This is in contrast to the "lower mind" of fearful thoughts, which make fear-based decisions.

If you will develop the automatic habit of consulting with your upper mind and God (who are one) to receive answers and guidance, and then following that guidance, you will peacefully walk upon the smooth pathway of love.

Prior to making decisions, pause for a moment and turn to God, Who is always available for guidance. This full access is a gift that you were given, and when you don't consult with God, you are missing the benefits of your gift.

Some humans choose not to ask God for help, because of concerns that God is too busy and they or their problems aren't important enough to warrant personal attention. This is a limiting belief that creates needless pain and suffering.

Imagine how your life would be different if you completely followed the guidance of God and your upper mind. Feel the deep peace envelop you as you realize this is a way of living that is akin to a return home to Heaven.

Your Creator, like any loving parent, always guides you to take the path of love in every situation. To the Creator, there are no other options but love.

Since your mind is already merged with God's mind, you already *do* hear the loving thoughts from God in your own mind. Whether or not this conversation is in your conscious awareness is your freewill choice.

Therefore, consulting with God doesn't mean looking externally to yourself, as you would search for a guru upon a mountaintop. God is right here, within your mind, as you are within God's mind. So, consulting simply means turning on the awareness of the loving voice that's within your mind. This is the gentle yet strong guidance that you can feel, see, know, and hear. This guidance makes perfect sense and rings true.

If you forget to consult with God prior to making a decision, we angels deliver strong guidance from

God—especially if you ask for our assistance. Our guidance, coupled with noticing your emotional body's feedback (for example, does the decision feel "off," or does it feel comfortable?), always leads you back to the path of love from whence you came.

The internal struggle of not knowing what to do arises when fear battles for control. Fear always argues and speaks in terms of worst-case scenarios, like a poor, panicked, caged animal. How can this force be trusted to create, when the creation is always a reflection of its creator? To consult fear before making decisions is to guarantee endless drama and suffering.

Even the term *surrender* or *let go* creates more anxiety on the fear-based path, because fear is obsessed with being in control. To the ego, surrender is the equivalent of losing to the enemy, and admitting weakness and defeat.

How very differently does your upper mind see surrender! Now we are defining *surrender* as sinking into the deliciously comfortable folds of God's love. Upon the pathway of love, surrender is the same as "relaxing."

And it *is* relaxing to surrender everything to God and your upper mind. No more struggles or second-guessing, just a smooth pathway upon which you effortlessly glide with complete confidence.

The ego fears that it will lose its individuality or personality if it surrenders to God, because the ego has no recollection of the delicious merging with God that is your true spiritual home. The ego has no idea what it's like to feel safe, comfortable, and accepted. To the ego, "you" are the embodiment of its fears, and to lose these fears would be to lose its very life force.

It's not advisable to get into a tug-of-war match with the ego, where you attempt to wrest control away from the fearful one. The ego loves competitiveness and is obsessed with winning. Instead of struggling to overcome fear so that you can surrender an issue to God, send love to that part of you that is struggling.

Send love to the ego.

Send love to fear energy.

Send love to that part of you that feels afraid.

Send love to your fear of surrender, and your desire to be in control.

Have compassion for your dream of separation, born of a fantasy about running the universe. Fear always melts away in the presence of unconditional love and compassionate understanding. Like pouring water upon a fire, love cools anger, anxiety, guilt, and other offshoots of fear.

Think of a loving mother comforting her crying infant, and you will sense the energy of compassion to extend to your own self . . . including your ego.

Surrender to loving yourself as God loves you: completely. Love your physical, emotional, intellectual, and energetic bodies, and listen to them compassionately. Just don't take advice from them without first consulting with God.

If you miscreate with fear energy, you can always ask God for a ladder to climb back up to love. This is where we see prayer's effectiveness, in switching the channels from fear to love so that healing can occur. Don't try to fix anything by your lower self, when your upper self is always available for solutions.

God is continuously connected and available, and it's impossible to "bother" or "upset" God. The merged union you eternally enjoy with God gives you complete access to the infinite library of information.

It's so much easier to consult God ahead of making a decision, rather than praying for a miracle after taking a detour along the path of fear. Why not avoid problems in the first place by habitually consulting with Divine wisdom prior to taking action?

Surrendering Back into God

For most humans, there's heartbreak when you realize that lasting and fulfilling happiness cannot be found externally. You could celebrate the most perfect achievement, purchase the most perfect product, eat the most perfect meal, and get accolades from the whole world, and these externals still wouldn't lead to lasting happiness or fulfillment.

Perhaps these externals offer brief moments of satisfaction, but they cannot last—nor can they be pieced together to create one long interlude of happiness. You can enjoy a savory meal, which is far different from relying upon that meal to give you meaning and fulfillment. To do so will lead to addictively eating in order to attain the sense of satisfaction. The same holds true with other forms of addiction.

This is your moment of giving up the external search and realizing that this world holds nothing that will fulfill you in the same way that you remember Heaven's fulfillment. There's a grieving process that occurs when you realize that you've wasted time chasing after futile goals that will never pay off. Sadness, and even a sense that your whole world is crashing down around you, can make you feel vulnerable and unsure of yourself.

This process and these feelings are part of the undoing effect when you release the ego's attachments to synthetic replacements for Heaven. The gaudy temple that was built to glorify the ego comes crashing down.

Facing this "dark night of the soul" and the accompanying heartbreak leads to the blessing of opening your heart to the true Source of lasting happiness and fulfillment. This is what surrender means: giving up the external search for happiness, and returning to relaxing in the comfortable folds of God's love.

This is when you return to Heaven and your Heavenly consciousness, while still having your earthly body and life. You dedicate the rest of your mortal life to selflessness, realizing that this is the only path that replicates the oneness and happiness of Heaven.

You still continue with the dream of living in a separated physical body; however, instead of expending your earthly resources upon futile pursuits, you devote yourself to meaningful and selfless service. By helping other people, animals, the environment, and so forth, you help yourself to feel fulfilled and truly happy. Spend that same amount of time, money, and energy that you would have used for a temporary pleasure to instead enjoy the lasting fulfillment of knowing that you contributed. And in giving, so do you always receive that which matters.

7

God Is Happiness

A Message about Answered Prayers

We have seen confusion occur when a person realizes the futility of looking outwardly for happiness. They then begin to look inwardly, and the search for happiness continues.

So let us clarify that any form of looking, searching, or seeking—whether outwardly or inwardly—is a denial that happiness is already here. Dear One, you do not need to look for that which is here. There's no need to search inwardly to find a "hidden" treasure, when what you seek is displayed openly for you now.

Let us circle back to the beginning, when God created you in the image and likeness of all that is God:

— **God is happiness.** Therefore, you don't *have* happiness, which implies a separate possession—you *are* happiness. Happiness is your true identity, and who you really are right now and always.

So if you don't feel happy, this is identical to not feeling like yourself. You can't lose happiness, because *it is you*. However, you can lose touch with reality and believe that you're unhappy, which really means *un*-you.

There's no need to complicate happiness, inner peace, health, or any other quality. *Looking for happiness at a shopping mall is identical to searching for happiness at a seeking-focused spirituality class.* They are both illustrations of not accepting that you already are happy, peaceful, fulfilled, and so forth.

Seeking within is still seeking, and the process of seeking takes you away from the experience of being. True stillness, in contrast, is *enjoying* the present-moment magnificence of the love, the depth of satisfaction, and the power of the gifts that you are. How can you enjoy something when you are seeking it? Stop seeking and enjoy who you are.

— **God is peace.** Therefore, you don't need to meditate for hours, read countless books, travel to exotic locations, publish your writing, have a healing practice, or do anything else in order to be at peace. You already *are* at peace, because that is who you are.

— **God is health.** Therefore, you don't need to seek healing in the future, but enjoy your health in the present moment . . . and then experience that you are healthy.

— **God is love.** Therefore, you are love, loving, loved, and lovable. The entirety of God, encompassing every person, loves you completely and unconditionally.

— **God is fulfillment.** God has no needs, nor do you. Within the dream of having a separate physical body, everything is opposite to the reality of Heaven:

- In spiritual truth, you are one with God. In the dream, you are separated from God.

- In spiritual truth, you are one with every being. In the dream, you have separate bodies.

- In spiritual truth, you have no needs. In the dream, you must work to meet your needs.

- In spiritual truth, you share loving harmony with everyone. In the dream, egos clash and compete.

The dream of separation from God is terrifying, because it's a disconnection from Source that has thrust you into a bizarre and opposite world. You can never feel safe or relax into enjoying your Godly self in a place where fear is treated as royalty.

What you can do, though, is utilize your Godly self—and all of the God-power who you are—to bend the dream into a more fulfilling and pleasant experience.

The Power That God Created as You

We've repeatedly emphasized that the physical human experience is a realistic dream that you're having, while you're back home in Heaven asleep in the comfortable folds of God's love. The dream began with the idea that you could take your God-given power of creation and make your own world where "you" were in charge. Thus began the ego—the seemingly opposing will to God.

So are you trapped within this dream? Is physical death the only escape from the dream? The answer to both questions is *no*.

Just as in a nightly sleeping dream where you can direct the outcome, so too can you direct the dream of separation.

By "directing," we are not implying that you would control everyone and everything. Although you are as powerful as God created you, the desire to control the world is one more example of seeking happiness through external situations. Being "Ruler of the World" is an attempt to feel loved (which you already are) and special (which is a goal of the separated ego, which wants other people to be better or worse than itself to maintain the illusion of separation).

Perhaps it's best to continue the analogy of the dreams you have when you are sleeping. You'd probably agree that some dreams are pleasant, while others are upsetting nightmares. Then there are lucid dreams, in which you are aware that you're dreaming. During lucid dreams, you can make conscious decisions to change the plot and direction of the dream. In this way, you can explore fantastic experiences such as levitating and flying, morphing and shape-shifting, enjoying romantic interludes, and so forth.

It is the same with the dream of separation. Once you become aware of the fact that you are actually back home in Heaven, dreaming that you're in a separated physical body, then you can consciously make decisions to alter the plot and direction of the dream.

God didn't just *give* you power—God *made* you power. You *are* the power that can have, be, achieve, and do anything. You have no limits—none.

Your life is now a lucid dream, in which you are the director. The question becomes: In what direction do you wish to direct your dream?

For many, the wish is toward the acquisition of external possessions and experiences. And you *can* have this experience and accumulate as much as you desire. This in itself can be a catalyst for understanding that—no matter how much you achieve and receive—there's a lingering emptiness. No amount of riches, food, college degrees, relationships, titles, or awards can fill the emptiness.

This is the point in the dream when we pray you will choose true fulfillment, instead of endless emptiness. Please hear us: You absolutely can have a safe, comfortable, and fulfilling dream life. You have the God-given power to instantly create whatever you need *as a platform* for your selfless service. God doesn't will that you be a pauper while you help others, because God does not see lack in any way. To imply that if you receive, another doesn't receive, is to affirm lack and limitations—neither of which exists except upon the path of fear.

So, your dream of separation can be as pleasant as any happy dream you've experienced while sleeping. Use your God-power to experience a delightful path of love. Have a loving family, a comfortable home, wonderful health, and everything else considered desirable. But do not believe that those experiences lead to the deep fulfillment you recall from your Heavenly life.

Those pleasant experiences are your backdrop, not your foreground. Be not obsessed with your home, possessions, work, or finances, but be in gratitude for all that you've chosen to have. You directed this lucid dream, and you can choose to change the plot and direction.

We've discussed the paths of love and fear, and how your creations from selfless love are lasting and satisfying, and your creations from selfishness and desires to be better than others (separate from others) are short-lived and unsatisfying.

The True Nature of Prayer

You, who have all of the power of the universe at your disposal, should not limit yourself to little tricks of manifesting magic. This can be a magnificent masterpiece dream, with an inspiring and happy plot.

The means of directing your movie-like dream are through prayer. Most think of prayer as appealing to a faraway committee, who may or may not approve your request. Superstitious rituals to appeal to God's mercy are thereby developed.

We see an unconscious resistance to prayer, much like teenagers who resent having to ask their parents for car keys. So it is soothing to realize that prayer is not appealing to a separate authority figure—because God is within your mind and you are within God's mind. Your loving thoughts are literally God's thoughts moving through you.

Prayer is choosing.

Prayer is directing.

Prayer is deciding what the next scene in your dream movie will be.

Do you need God's permission to direct and decide? This concern stems from seeing God as a distant authority figure, which is a habitual belief that may take a while to replace with the following realizations:

There is no separation between you and God: you are forever merged;

and

God created you with the power to create.

That being said, you have the power to create from fear or to create from love. Anything created from love is lasting and satisfying. Anything created from fear is within the unreal dream of separation, and therefore can neither last nor bring fulfillment.

God does not punish, block, test, or withhold; however, you can use your God-given power to create fear-based punishments, blocks, tests, and trials. You have the power to direct a movie that is a tragedy, a comedy, or an inspiring masterpiece with your choices.

So rather than asking for permission to have your prayers granted, ask for guidance about what to create.

Consulting with God prior to making a decision is identical to consulting with your higher self or the Holy Spirit—in other words, asking for directions to the path of love.

Sometimes, though, fear is so pervasive that lifting your thoughts to God may seem impossible. That's when you can call upon Jesus, us angels, or other beings of pure love, to elevate your consciousness.

Make no mistake: God hears and feels you, whether you're in the midst of fear or in the glory of love. There is never a time when your prayers are unheard or ignored.

However, when your thoughts are clouded and your emotions numbed, you may not hear God's wisdom or feel God's warm love. That's when turning to Jesus or us angels can lift you to the level of love, and remind you to consult God's wisdom for *everything*.

When you pray for other people, you are choosing and directing your desires for them. Always remember, though, that other people are also choosing and directing their own dream. So a prayer for someone else may not result in your desired direction, because each individual within the dream of separation is directing and choosing their own dream.

We emphasize this because we see many humans fall from faith when it seems that their prayers aren't answered. They pray for someone's health, and the person instead succumbs. Remember that the path of fear is to blame, and that includes "blaming" God for someone's seemingly untimely passing.

Within the separation dream, blame is a commonplace occurrence. It helps humans to deflect guilt they may harbor and to make sense of their experiences.

Yet, the separation dream is occurring inside every seemingly separate mind. You and all others are choosing and directing a separate "movie plot" within the dream. This is where the belief in free will comes from.

Let us say that you are the one praying for a person to heal from a medical condition, and the person does not heal and succumbs instead. Would you "blame" God for not hearing your prayer? How could this be when every prayer is heard and answered?

What if your movie plot differs from that of the person for whom you're praying? Any person with serious health challenges is shown their various potential outcomes and choices by their guardian angels. So the person in this example may have been shown that, if he chose to survive physically, his family would have to medically care for him. And then he was shown an alternative of leaving his physical body, and how his family would grieve but ultimately would be "relieved of the burden" of his caretaking. So he chooses to leave the physical dream, because he believes that's the most loving gift to bestow upon his family. That is his choice.

Could he have chosen a third option of recovering completely, and living physically with his family without the need for their care? Of course! Everything is possible with your power of choice. We will next discuss why humans would choose a path considered less than optimal.

8

The Light of Awakening

A Message about Choices

Arriving at a fully conscious awareness of oneness with God is a process:

- *First*, a spark of intellectual curiosity, perhaps after hearing or reading a discussion of oneness.

- *Second*, contemplation about this possibility and the implications.

- *Third*, a mystical experience that arouses curiosities about God's closeness.

- *Fourth*, a shift from fearing God to being aware of the pleasant intoxication of God's love.

- *Fifth*, a firm belief in the oneness of God, but still with a viewpoint of being separated from God.

- *Sixth,* more frequent experiences of seeing everyone as one with you.

- *Seventh,* a desire to return to oneness consciousness, accompanied by fervent prayers, asking God to deliver you from the ego's separation dream.

- *Eighth,* fears about losing control are given to God, so that you can detach from the ego's dream of separation.

- *Ninth,* walking in both worlds simultaneously—seeing the separated world of the ego as a dream, and having compassion for those who are dreaming.

- *Tenth,* developing the habit of consulting God and your higher self before making decisions.

- *Eleventh,* feeling and experiencing God's love continuously. Earthly life feels joyous.

- *Twelfth,* teaching others by your positive example to trust in God.

This is not a list by which to measure "spiritual accomplishments," as the ego would like to do. This is merely a generalized road map of the arc from the moment of falling asleep to the moment of awakening.

We angels are egoless and have no attachment to when or how you awaken. Our only focus is upon reminding you of your true Divine nature—knowledge that automatically brings with it happiness and a sense of safety.

Facing the Fears of Awakening

If you were to awaken a friend who was having a nightmare, there would be confused moments of disbelief that the nightmare wasn't real. So it is with our human companions to whom we are assigned.

We witness the light of awakening soon followed by the dimming darkness of forgetfulness, the paths of love and fear oscillating like a roller coaster, until at last the decision is made to choose stability with true and lasting happiness.

When we angels promise you a peaceful life filled with love for yourself, all others, and of course God, we are handing you the key to all that you desire. There is no cost nor sacrifice for this . . . except to the ego, which quivers at the idea of losing control.

What fears arise when you think about completely surrendering to God? The fear of being controlled, being ridiculed, relinquishing your individuality, or missing out on material fun? These fears are the marionette strings the ego pulls in order to control you.

The ego warns that you will lose the pleasures of life, as well as your individuality, if you turn your life over to God. "Life will be boring, no one will admire you, and you won't have any money," says the ego.

The voice of fear speaks to your "Achilles' heel," as well. That is, your personal fears and vulnerabilities. So, if you fear that people will leave you, laugh at you, fire you, and so forth, those are the specific examples the ego will mirror to you. The ego always speaks in worst-case scenarios, pretending to be your intuition warning you about a dire future.

The voice of fear claims that those who surrender to God's will are destined to lead an ascetic life of impoverishment. Let us recall that "surrender" really means joyfully consulting with God to ensure that your actions are aligned with love, not fear.

From this perspective, we see that the happiest people are those who have harmonious lives. Their income levels vary, as do their accomplishments. Yet, they all share a common thread of devoting their lives to joy: living an exuberant existence with gratitude and blessings, and spreading joy wherever they go.

The fear of loss of control is really the fear of being told what to do. The ego is a rebel who doesn't want any advice, thinks guidance is akin to criticism, and views consulting with anyone as a sign of weakness. Ironically, though, the ego has no problem telling you what to do. If you don't comply, it punishes you with fear.

The ego wants you to be a separate universe, with it as king and you as its subject. It warns that you will lose this fragile kingdom if you betray it by going to God for guidance.

Yet there is no other choice, because happiness is who you are. To choose other than happiness is to extend the dream of separation and walk upon the path of fear. Think of worry as an admission ticket to the path of fear.

In the topsy-turvy physical world of separation, the ego's arguments seem logical and lead to the fears that prevent you from consulting with God. We will list and explain these fears as a way of exposing them to the light of understanding, so that fear will dissipate just as darkness disappears once a light is turned on.

— **Deservingness and worthiness.** A deep-seated concern about being "good enough" to garner love and help from God, Jesus, and the angels comes from focusing upon the separated you, which is the unreal you. The separated self feels fundamentally flawed, because you know that it's not who you really are. However, when you are consulting God, you are your true self who feels natural and comfortable. You love yourself in a healthy and balanced way, so you know that you—like everyone—deserve God's help and support. You are just as deserving and worthy as everyone else, because God created you purposefully. Always remember that you are within God, and God is within you.

— **Abandonment.** Abandonment fears are triggered by the original separation dream. The ego has convinced you that God is far away, and that you are alone and abandoned, with only the ego as your ally. Yet, you could never be separated from God, except within the dream. However, the original shock of feeling apart from God is perceived as the ultimate parental abandonment. Until you face these fears, they remain hidden and are replicated in abandonment experiences within the dream, like mirrors into mirrors into mirrors, the endless reflection of the original wound. The fear of consulting God comes from the fear that you have abandoned God, or that God has abandoned you—both of which are impossible.

— **Social isolation or rejection.** *What will people think?* is a major concern of the ego, which jockeys for the position of being better than others. The ego is obsessed with being above others, as a way of maintaining the illusion of separation. The fear is that consulting with God may lead one to make unpopular choices, akin to running away and becoming a hermit. If your family and friends aren't spiritually minded, you may worry that they'll judge you. In the separated dream, those who consult with God experience a period of letting go of anything artificial, including relationships that are no longer symbiotic. This is part of the awakening, exactly like the transition from your nightly dreams to the moment when you open your eyes in the morning.

— **Resistance to change.** As you shift from the path of fear to walking the path of love, changes inevitably occur. It's akin to turning the lights on and seeing a mess that you didn't notice in the dark. Now that you know there's a mess, you want to clean it up. And so it is with when you realize that you can turn to God for everything and receive trustworthy and brilliant guidance. Suddenly, your standards rise, because God has high standards for everyone. You're no longer willing to settle and suffer, so you consider making changes. The question is whether you trust God's guidance. Your relationships change as well, as you become more spiritually focused. You and your friends may not share interests anymore and may grow apart. In the separation dream, grief normally accompanies change. There's grieving for what was, and the letting-go process.

— **Financial insecurity.** *If I surrender to God's will, does this mean I will impulsively quit my job and not have an income?* Such is the fear of consulting with God. It's the fear of the unknown future and giving up control to "someone else's will." Just remember that your will and God's will are one. By surrendering to God, you're actually surrendering to your own higher self's will instead of the ego's will of fear. We find that when humans surrender to God, they become more relaxed and assured, and thereby find more satisfaction and "success" with work.

— **Perfectionism and procrastination.** Feeling stuck is often a sign of perfectionism, where you're afraid of making the "wrong" decision. This results in a fear of moving forward, lest you choose actions that you later regret. Very often, perfectionism is an unconscious belief that someone will judge you for your choices, or for not performing up to some unrealistically high standard. Ultimately, it's the ego doing the judging, and since the ego is an unreal illusion, there is nothing to fear. While it's wise to consult God before making decisions and taking action, once you have your Divine assignment, you can move forward confidently—always checking in with God along the way.

— **Losing control.** We see many humans who fear that surrendering to God means that they'll "go crazy" and exhibit bizarre behavior. This is because they believe the path of fear keeps them safe, and the path of love is frivolous or naïve.

— **Giving up power.** The ego is always fighting against "enemies" who might take away its power and control. The ego imagines that it is struggling with God to see who is in charge of you. So the idea of surrendering to God is akin to defeat to the ego. Of course, this power struggle is purely within the dream of separation . . . and it can play out among people within the dream. Engaging in power struggles is always draining and futile, because no one can control the Holy Child of God who you are in spiritual truth.

There are other variations of these fears the ego creates in order to keep you convinced that you are separate from God and other people. Now that you've seen the illogical nature of these fears, they cannot grip you as before. We angels can help to untangle you from the web of egoic fears, as you request us to. Simply say the word, and we are there with you to lift away the veil and help you to remember who and where you are in spiritual truth.

While you're still in physical form, we can help you to enjoy a happy dream upon the path of love. It's still a dream, because it still appears that you are in a separated body . . . but you see through this illusion, and notice the bright, glowing Divine light of God within yourself and everyone you meet. This is beyond the process of forgiving, because you only see love instead of the surface illusions.

Recall a time when you made a decision clearly and easily. There was a knowingness that it was the right choice. You made it, and never looked back. Choosing to have a happy dream is no more complicated than that. In fact, it's easier, because in spiritual truth there's nothing to decide. You are merely choosing to be consciously aware of the fact that you already are happy.

In the dream of separation, shifting from a fearful dream to a happy dream is a matter of making the choice to do so. You are choosing to be your true self, which doesn't even require a choice because you already are your true self.

Say: "I choose to have a happy dream," with sincerity in your physical, emotional, intellectual, and energetic bodies, and you are awakened to a new dream—still separated, yet happy and peaceful.

Sticking with Your Choice

Just as the master teacher Jesus once demonstrated, temptation abounds to slip back onto the path of fear. Some will call this impulse *the devil, evil, darkness, ego,* or *lower energies.* Regardless of the theological orientation, all are speaking of the lure to return to the path of fear.

Within the dream of separation, your physical, emotional, intellectual, and energetic bodies become easily distracted by attempts to fulfill their needs. It's tempting to engage in competition, for example, to earn enough money to buy food, housing, and other essentials. In the separated dream, everything is lacking. So you need to compete for the few resources available.

In spiritual truth, there is an abundance of everything, and plenty to spare. So, competition is not considered an option. You can earn money while on the path of love by choosing a career that involves offering benevolent services or products at fair prices. We will soon discuss more about how to stay upon the path of love "in this world."

Back home in Heaven with God, all of your needs are fulfilled . . . because, like a child in the womb, you really don't *have* any needs while merged with God. You are instantly and continuously fulfilled.

Lest you think that an easy way to find happiness is to destroy your physical body, please understand that we are discussing consciousness, not physicality. Many people who transition from physical to spiritual lives through passing over are still obsessed with the path of fear. Human physical death is not a magical panacea for spiritual growth. There are many levels of consciousness, and *the choice of focusing upon love or fear is the same for those who are in physical bodies and for those who have left their physical bodies.*

In other words, physical death is not an instant path to peace. Your consciousness still survives and continues its same focus and habits, such as worry, anger, unforgiveness, and guilt. We angels counsel all who desire our help to attune their thoughts to oneness instead of separation.

It is only through knowing and feeling that all is one that complete, consistent, and lasting peace occurs.

The Role of Boredom

Boredom is one of the primary temptations we see pulling humans from a love consciousness to a fear consciousness. There's an experience of angst when humans realize that pursuing meaningless goals will never lead to peace or happiness. *What shall I do instead?* is the natural existential question that arises when you turn your focus to that which matters.

When you cease worrying what others will think, there's no need to accumulate or acquire. There's no need to impress others, because that's the insecure path of fear. So once you stop competing, chasing, acquiring, and engaging in other ego-based habits, there's often an interim period of grief and confusion. Grief as your old habits, which brought some semblance of comfort, are no longer needed. Confusion as you wonder what your next step is.

The ego is relentless in its unquenchable thirst to control you, especially if you've now devoted your life to a benevolent, helpful purpose. The ego casts shadows over those who threaten its reign. If your focus will inspire others to also live from love instead of fear, then the ego must target you to assure its own livelihood.

The only weapon the ego has available is fear. Any fears you've hidden from conscious awareness are the secret ones the ego will use to convince you to join it. The ego will convince you that something awful will occur unless you "protect yourself" by being afraid and looking for additional fears. That's why we emphasize the importance of facing fears, with the same compassion for yourself that caring parents would have toward their crying infant.

So let's use an example of you devoting yourself to selfless aid of others, charitable work, or a beneficial service or product that you will offer at a fair price. Perhaps you decide to conduct healing work, write a book, or help children. These are examples, and there are many other ways to work upon the path of love.

As you devote yourself to your love-based work, the ego—being fear itself—becomes afraid that your love-based work will take away its fear-based control over other people. So the ego looks for your secret fears, and convinces you that they will come true if you continue upon your love path. The ego says that you will lose something or someone that is valuable to you, unless you join its hypervigilant focus upon fear.

This results in distractions while conducting your love-based work, and you find yourself bored and uninspired to continue. Boredom means that your mind and heart aren't engaged in your love-based project, and you spend your time and energy on other activities. Meanwhile your project is ignored, so it doesn't flourish.

The boredom is a sign of walking upon the path of fear. It means that you are on a different wavelength from your project. The ego is asking you to find instant fulfillment and happiness (which it cannot offer to you) through meaningless activities.

So instead of being directed toward something that's meaningful to you, your time and attention are deflected toward something that is temporarily exciting but which doesn't hold lasting meaning. In other words, the ego uses fear to switch your focus to external pursuits of happiness and fulfillment.

And now we will reveal the ego's primary mode of operation: attempting to convince you that if you take fear-based actions, you will be elevated above other people. It says that this object will win you prestige, and that this action will win you awards. It steers you toward "making other people jealous" and "success is the best revenge" paths—with the express intention of keeping the dream of separation alive.

The ego will always ask you to see yourself as better than others or worse than others. It really doesn't care if you consider yourself *above* or *below* other people. All it cares about is keeping the illusion of separation intact.

And so the ego's distractions are synthetic substitutes for genuine paths of happiness. True satisfaction cannot be "won," because it's already given. And "making other people jealous" of you is a cold, lonely, and distancing avenue.

You could garner the entire world's applause, praise, or envy and still feel empty and unhappy. Contrast this with how it feels to help those in genuine need or to inspire others to lift up their own consciousness to love.

Boredom means that you don't fully believe in your ability to bring your love-based project to fruition. And yet, if you were Divinely guided to begin this project, then you will be Divinely guided each step of the way. God works through everyone who focuses upon lovingly serving. Place your confidence in God within, and self-doubt is eradicated.

You'll recognize boredom by the restlessness it engenders. There's a panicked need to find the key to happiness, and—like someone moving through television channels rapidly—ego-induced boredom is anxious to find what it's looking for. Yet, it doesn't even *know* what it's looking for. The ego promises: "You'll know that this is 'it' when you find it," without giving any clues to what is being sought. The ego only promises relief from boredom for those who enter the race of looking for the key to happiness.

Restless boredom is the antithesis of peace, because the idea of peace enrages the ego. The ego uses a manipulative marketing scheme to convince you that peace is boring. "Look at those peaceful people," the ego loudly whispers. "They aren't doing anything exciting. You don't want to be like them." The ego glosses over the observation that the peaceful people are happy so that you'll focus only upon their gentle actions.

Once the ego has you convinced that peace is boring (and therefore the worst possible outcome), it can then easily tempt you with drama. The path of fear and drama is filled with habitual arguing ("sport fighting"), competing, leaving behind your love-based projects, self-sabotage, and other fear-based actions.

The ego's world is completely focused upon winning at any cost. There's no sense that taking from another or acting in hurtful ways is the same as taking from or hurting yourself. The ego believes in the splintered illusion of separation and does not see that what you do to another, you do to yourself.

If you are paying attention, you notice that each "mirage" the ego tries to tempt you with is a pathway to misery, suffering, and poverty. There is no experience, object, or circumstance the ego can usher you toward that will result in anything but more emptiness.

The ego doesn't want you to see this painful pattern. It says, "This time will be different. If you can acquire or achieve this one 'external,' then you'll finally be happy. *This* one will finally bring joy. This is the real key to happiness, *promise.*"

Release yourself from the grips of the ego's invitation to misery, Dear One, and see through its empty claims and futile pursuits. *The realization that nothing outside of you will make you happy is the key to happiness*—a topic we will now explore further with you.

9

Peaceful Excitement

A Message about Real Fulfillment

Just as nothing external can make you happy, so can nothing external make you sad, angry, or afraid. The true you lives in the peaceful eye of the drama-filled hurricane of the dream of separation. You are unscathed by time, stress, or aging, and you are exactly as God originally created you: timeless and outside of time.

Without the measurement of time, there is no past, present, or future with which to compare yourself. There are no goals or mountains to climb, no gray hairs or wrinkles to count, and no circumstances to plan for. All is completely blissful enjoyment of the pervasive love nourishing and supporting you. This is the real you, and your real life.

You don't need to acquire knowledge, which implies that knowledge is outside of you and must be pursued and captured. There is nothing outside of you.

To the ego, this sounds boring and unchallenging. Yet, is an infant bored while being cradled in a loving parent's arms? All the drama of the world derives from one error in thinking: that you are separate from others and must compete with them for what you need. When you see this drama for what it is, you won't need to participate.

There is a quieter form of excitement that peace offers to you, while you are in the dream of having a physical body. You are in the dream now, walking upon the path of love, with full awareness that there is no separation between you and other people, us angels, Jesus, or God.

While the world's trinkets and dramas promise relief from boredom, and a way to distract yourself from your love-based projects, the truth is that these externals only offer a meager substitute for lasting happiness. Externals always disappoint, falling short of the promise they hold.

Imagine waking up each morning, instead, with an exciting sense of belonging, meaning, and purpose. We angels do help in this regard, by shifting your perspective away from *What can I gain?* to *How may I serve?* The first is the ego's motto, and the second is the call of your soul.

Denying or escaping the world is the same as affirming the reality of the dream of the world. Any obsession with *leaving* the world is exactly like the obsession with being better than others *in* the world. They are all forms of separation thinking, which perpetuates believing that you are removed from God and other people. As we've discussed, this belief in separation is the basis of suffering.

Suffering is not God's will, as God is pure happiness. There is no part of God's consciousness that includes suffering. If it seems that God ignores suffering, it is because God is unaware of anything but the spiritual truth of pure love. The illusions cannot enter into a mind that is 100 percent love.

This is why God sent Jesus and us angels to awaken those who are asleep to Divine love. We enter into the dream of separation and firmly take your hand to pull you upward and out of the nightmare. The ego is terrified of God, Jesus, and angels, viewing us as competition in the pursuit of control and victory.

To Heavenly beings, there is no competition, as nothing has changed since all was originally created . . . except in a very realistic dream.

Bringing Joy to Physical Living

Since you understand that physical living is a very realistic dream, you can use the power that God created in you to influence the dream. It's similar to someone asking you, "If you could snap your fingers and create the life of your dreams, what would you do and change?" Well, we angels are telling you that you don't need to snap your fingers to shift the direction of your dream.

As we've mentioned, waking dreams and sleeping dreams are identical projections of your intellectual body. The example we gave earlier of a "lucid dream" shows how you have the power to make conscious choices while dreaming. During a sleeping lucid dream, you can decide to change a negative story line into a positive one. Lucid dreams generally involve you asserting yourself and saying "No!" to intrusions upon your peace.

This is exactly the process of taking charge of your waking dream. Being aware that "life is but a dream" means that you are the dreamer who influences the dream experience. You have the option of consulting with God about every decision, and then taking the time to hear the answers.

You approach life as if you were part of a Heavenly team of scriptwriters. The more you consult with God prior to writing your script, the happier the movie.

Now, the ego takes a "kid in a candy store" approach to the power God has created in you. To the ego, this is carte blanche license to *take, take, take.* And taking certainly is an option, with all of the power God bestowed in you. However, solely taking does not lead to happiness. *You do remember how it feels to be truly happy, and you still feel happiness in spiritual truth.* What blocks your awareness of happiness is the obsession with acquiring more. This sets the mind to believing that you are not enough, and that you will only feel whole through finding something to fulfill you—which is a depressing thought indeed.

The ego would have you suffer at a meaningless job in order to pay for your acquisitions. To the ego, suffering is the path to happiness and "spiritual growth." Yet, how could one who is already merged with God's mighty mind need to acquire more knowledge or growth?

You are awakening from the illusion of separation into the sure knowledge that you are forever one with God.

Recognizing Needs and Wants

The way out is to be aware of the difference between a need and a want:

- Look at externals as *needs* instead of wants. In the physical dream, you *need* food, water, shelter, and other basics, so you are looking to these externals for sustenance, not as the source of happiness or fulfillment. You acknowledge that it's pleasurable to eat a satisfying meal, but you don't make the meal the magical solution to problems. This way, you won't be disappointed when the external doesn't live up to unrealistic standards.

- This is in contrast to *wants*, in which you believe that something outside of yourself is the key to lasting happiness. There's the thought *If only I had this* [item, job, person, home, condition, etc.], *then I'd finally be happy.* Placing an external circumstance in charge of your happiness creates the illusion that you don't have the God-given power to choose happiness.

Many "wants" are a way to manage the stress that is part of the dream of separation and duality. What compulsive behaviors are you engaged in to avoid stress, but which are actually creating *more* stress for you? For instance, compulsive shopping, eating, or drinking are desires to merge with something external that you believe will fill you up and increase your happiness. The external seems to be the answer to stress management.

But please pause and consider whether the actions involved with acquiring this external are adding to your stress level. For instance, with shopping there are stressors involved with the acquisition: financing, transporting, maintaining, and protecting the item. Most of the time, it's the externals that begin to "own" and control you. This increases your stress levels, so you then seek the next external "prize" to lower your stress and increase your happiness.

Continuing this honest discussion, please consider whether any of the externals you may have chased after resulted in lasting happiness and inner peace. Then consider those times when you have felt completely at peace and deeply happy: Where were you, with whom, and what were you doing? Was the happiness momentary, or has it lasted?

These questions are not a form of judgment for your choices, but guidance for your self-inventory. Your experiences are your greatest teacher, which yield instant feedback as to whether the experiences engendered pain and fear, or peace and love. At first, you may not care whether you feel pain, or you may liken pain to excitement. And as you grow to love yourself as God loves you, you begin to care about yourself. This is when you choose loving and peaceful experiences, instead of those leading to pain and fear.

The painful experiences are often born of disappointments, because your expectations for the external "prize" to fulfill you weren't met. The pain of disappointment is a pattern in a long series of life events. If you consciously notice this pattern, you will no longer invest your future happiness within the mirage that a person, place, item, or situation will give you happiness.

Take a moment to consider how you would feel if you had fewer, instead of more, items to manage and care for. Would you feel free of entanglements? Less afraid of someone taking or breaking your belongings?

Then consider other externals you may have chased after, or tried to force into your life. Perhaps you suffered to earn the money for these externals, or in some other way placed yourself in harm's way. Did they yield the happiness and peace that you'd hoped?

These honest discussions with yourself can bring truth to conscious awareness. It's analogous to driving toward a specific destination. If happiness and peace are your intended destinations, you'll want to drive upon a road that leads you there. The best way to know if you're on the right path is to examine if your past actions yielded your desired results. If not, then you will need to change to a different set of actions.

Your road of happiness and peace is paved with simplicity. Instead of suffering to afford or chase after "wants," your focus is upon fulfilling your "needs." As we've discussed, you need basic provisions to maintain your physical body. Your intellectual, emotional, and energetic bodies also have basic needs of stimulation and attention.

Beyond these needs are the "wants," which usually involve an ego-based intention. For example, the ego "wants" prestigious items to impress others. This is a sign of viewing other people through the lens of duality, as if they are better or worse. Whenever there's a desire to "win" someone's attention or affection, it always originates from the ego attempting to maintain the illusion of separation.

We cannot emphasize this enough:

Whenever you view another person as below you in prestige, wealth, education, likability, intelligence, lovability, spirituality, attractiveness, consciousness, awareness, or any other measure, you are traveling upon the road of fear, loneliness, and misery. There are no advantages to being better than someone else, or "making them jealous of you." Being above someone is an illusion of being separated. How can you feel loved, when you see yourself as apart from others who would be your friends in the dream of separation?

Similarly, seeing others as better than you may be called "humility" by the ego, which is a master of disguising its fear-ridden methods. Yet, examine this humility, and you see this truth: *Whenever you view yourself as worse or less than, or below another person, you are emphasizing the illusion of the separation, and doubting God's purposeful creation who is you.*

Each time you judge yourself or another person (regardless of who they are or what they've done), you cast yourself onto the road of fear, pain, and misery. There is no escaping this fact because, in spiritual truth, you are forever merged with and equal to every other thought of God.

The ego wants to justify judgments against those who commit "unforgiveable acts." Yet, we cannot emphasize enough the high cost of holding even one judgment—no matter how justifiable it seems.

Let us revisit an earlier discussion about the difference between judgment and discernment. Judgment, as you recall, is the fuel of the ego as it casts labels of "good" or "bad" onto people. Always remember that the ego's basis of being is to maintain the illusion of you being separated from God and other people. In order to maintain this illusion, the ego must continually point out examples of other people being above or below you.

So judgments are the way that the ego interacts with the world of illusions. In contrast, your higher self is aware of oneness, and so uses the practice of discernment to initiate actions. Discernment means that you are either drawn to something, or you're not.

As an example, the ego would label someone who is heavily drinking alcohol and smoking cigarettes as "bad" or "less than." The ego would puff itself up with pride from this comparison. Yet, the ego is never happy. It is perpetually afraid—and associating yourself with the ego's thought system only ensures the same for you. There are no exceptions to this.

In comparison, the higher self would view the same person who is abusing alcohol and cigarettes with compassionate concern for their health and welfare. Instead of saying that the substance abuse is "bad," discernment would say, "I am not attracted to that behavior," or "I will pray for their health or happiness." Discernment would either avoid the substance-abusing person, or attempt to help them. No judgments involved, just action.

Now, the ego may try to help the substance-abusing person in order to gain accolades, appreciation, or applause. Remember that the ego is always trying to get something, because it views itself as flawed and lacking. The higher self says there is no separation between you and another person, so when you help another, you are helping yourself.

As long as you know this truth—*I am forever and completely one with God and every creation of God*—then you will not wander into judgments or the pursuit of "wants." Your life enjoys the quiet excitement of feeling loved and lovable. Your needs are simple and easily met.

10

The "Prize" of Life

A Message about Lasting Happiness

It is impossible to be afraid and happy simultaneously, as they are two energies that never intersect. We've used the metaphor before of the red and purple bands of the rainbow that never touch. The vibration of the color red is much too low to ever reach the high vibration of the color purple. It's the same with fear and happiness.

We can see that you would much prefer to enjoy the higher and lighter energies. We are continuously lifting you up, and whispering reminders of loved-based choices that you can make. We will now list some of the ways that you can stay in that lovely state of happiness, without having to vacillate between love and fear. This is a choice that you have each moment, which becomes easier once you are aware of these options and outlooks to sustain it.

- **Know that happiness is possible**. You were created happy, in God's happy image and likeness. Therefore, you already *are* happy in spiritual truth.

- **Feel that you deserve to be happy.** Your happiness is not taking away from anyone else, but is instead adding to the happiness of the world and uplifting everyone around you. Although you, like everyone, may feel a sense of guilt that makes you question your "deservingness," know that this guilt is purely from the ego. Any mistakes are learning opportunities.

- **Realize that happiness is your choice.** Nothing outside of you can "make" you happy. No person or object can create pure and lasting happiness within you. Happiness only occurs when you value happiness, know that it's attainable, realize that you deserve happiness, choose to be happy, and choose a happy outlook. This means seeing yourself, others, and your life through the lens of happiness.

- **Understand that happiness is your true self.** When you are happy, you are being yourself. Happiness gives you complete access to your God-given power.

- **Recognize the difference between your true self and the ego.** It's very simple: if you aren't happy, then you are operating from the ego's viewpoint, such as blaming or judging. The ego will tell you to go find happiness with an external such as a purchase, relationship, or consumable. These externals will give temporary and fleeting experiences of happiness, but only the true self's choice in favor of being happy leads to a pure and lasting state.

We will now focus upon helping you to recognize the ego's characteristics, and give you some methods that will restore you to your true self's happy outlook.

Purging Old Hurts

It seems that human life is fraught with hurt and disappointment. Any old resentments and regrets that you've been hauling around have created heaviness weighing you down from the higher vibrations.

Pointing the finger of blame toward yourself or another creates the illusion that you are separated individuals, which automatically places your consciousness upon the pathway of fear. Your mind can focus upon either duality or nonduality. So, if you view anyone as being to blame or "the problem," you will view yourself as separated from them. In that same moment, you also view yourself as alone and separated from God. This thought is the basis of all fear.

Hanging on to a past disturbance as a defensive safeguard against it occurring again is like carrying around a tack that punctured you long ago. You carry the tack as a reminder that this happened and to prevent you from stepping again upon another tack. Yet, carrying that tack is more harmful than the original injury!

Take a moment right now to quiet your mind and sense any masses in your energy field surrounding your body. Because if you're bitter about something that occurred in your past, you can be sure that you're carrying it around in an energy pouch right by your side, which will eventually assimilate into an unhealthful energy mass *within* you. So, there's an urgency in letting this old situation go . . . along with the bitterness and fears of it recurring.

The hurtful actions always arise from a belief in separation, with one person trying to "get" something from the other. The actions are selfish—which, as we've described, is the mentality that you must compete with other separated people to attain what you need, which you believe is only available in limited amounts.

You can purge hurts with this prayerful decision: *"I now release everything except for the lessons and the love."* Beneath the hurt lay love and trust that were betrayed, either by yourself or by another. That love always exists, whether or not the relationship continues. The energy of love is eternal and omnipresent, which means that it forever travels with you. This is true, even if you feel that you no longer love the person involved.

You are God's beloved creation, impervious to hurt because you were created as the unbreakable, immortal, and eternal extension of Divine love. In spiritual truth, no one and nothing can ever harm you. Your soul is forever alive. Yet, in the dream of separation, mounds of hurt can be stockpiled, which makes it difficult to remember your true Divine beingness.

Allow us angels to escort your consciousness Heavenward, bringing you back home in your awareness that all else is but a dream from which you are whisked away. Call upon us angels to help keep your focus upon the *eternal*, instead of the *external*.

Detaching from Ego

The ego is obsessed with analyzing other egos. It finds its own version of "pleasure" in dissecting motives, like a misguided detective. The only thing that the ego ever finds, however, is the path of fear and pain. Any analysis of egos is an affirmation of separation.

The intention is to understand why a person would behave the way they are behaving. Yet the answer is always the same, regardless of the details: A person is taking action either from the path of love or from the path of fear. Their action is either selfless (love) or selfish (fear).

The more you focus upon someone's egoic behavior or motives, the deeper you become mired with the heaviness of egoic energy. The basis of "drama addiction" is the desire to escape boredom and to achieve the approximation of meaningfulness.

If someone judges you, have compassion toward them for choosing the path of fear. They are pained by their decision to judge you and see you as separate. For you can be sure that this outlook of judgment is being cast widely, and not just upon you. *The habit of judging is the most painful addiction of them all.*

Always monitor yourself to notice if you are seeking a way to feel needed or entertained, as both are signals of the path of fear—which is the path of unfulfillment. Thousands of people could "need" you, yet you'd still feel lonely if it's an ego-connecting-with-ego relationship. As you notice this "need to be needed" or "need to be entertained," you will realize these are both *wants* instead of true *needs*.

The ego continuously seeks validation for its existence, including wanting to be needed, appreciated, and rewarded. Your true self, in contrast, gives for the pure joy of giving—without strings attached. The ego "knows" that it is not real, since fear is not real or God-created. So it is constantly worried that it will be discovered as an "impostor" or a "fraud." If you listen to the ego, it will try to convince you that *you* are an impostor or a fraud. Of course, you are not, but you can feel that way if you pretend to be someone other than your true spiritual self in an effort to be liked or accepted.

Your true self does not worry, and especially doesn't worry about acceptance or approval. Your true self is too busy loving everyone and everything. This is the key to detaching from the ego's tyrannical rule.

Fighting the ego, or feeling frustrated when you slip onto the path of fear, gives the ego the validation it seeks. You reinforce the ego's habits every time you berate yourself for feeling insecure.

Have compassion for yourself, and know that virtually every human occasionally slips into the ego's clutches. The key is to recognize when this occurs, and to detach from caring or worrying about the ego's dramas.

So you would say, for example, *I notice that I am currently feeling emotional pain, which means that I have allowed the ego to direct my thoughts. I now detach from worrying about this situation. I completely trust that by my detaching, the solution will rush in as quickly as flicking a light switch banishes all darkness.*

Detaching from the ego is not the same as being uncaring. In fact, it is more caring to detach than to pour the gasoline of worry upon the fire of egoic drama. Upon the path of love, you clearly receive your inner guidance about how best to provide selfless service that naturally helps others. Upon the path of fear, you engage in reactive rescuing where none is needed. In other words, the fear-based decisions are misguided and pull you away from true selfless service where it is genuinely needed.

Ask us for assistance in detaching from a situation in which you find yourself embroiled. We will help you detach from fears about others' judging you or taking something from you. We will reassure you that only the ego can judge, so it is an unreal illusion that can have no true impact. We will remind you that no one can take from you that which is yours.

Fear Is Not Entertainment

You are designed to be happy, so you feel best when you are happy. This may sound simple and obvious, but it bears repeating . . . especially since we see so many humans dragged into the smoke-and-mirrors illusion that it's entertaining to be afraid.

This illusion takes many forms, such as purposely watching a frightening movie or reading a suspenseful book. This edge-of-your-seat experience is the ego's version of happiness. The ego feels most alive when your heart is pounding and your mind is wondering what will happen next.

The ego is obsessed with predicting and controlling the future. While watching a frightening movie, you can witness its signature style whenever you feel angry at the movie characters for not foreseeing upcoming dangers. This is pure projection by the ego—which tries to control and foresee everything, which ironically creates and attracts danger and drama.

When you notice your reactions to various human activities, you can *feel* whether you're experiencing true lasting happiness, or a temporary respite from boredom. How do you feel when you are kind? When you are in a hurry? When you are participating in a fear-based experience?

There is wisdom to the phrase "Face your fears." The act of conquering fears by facing them is an ancient practice. Yet, there are two ways to face and conquer your fears, determined by the intention behind your actions.

First, there is the path of love, which views fear as a crying infant needing reassurance. Extend compassion toward yourself and others for feeling afraid. It's a case of amnesia, and forgetting your Divine spiritual power to create and uncreate.

Beware of any tendencies to reinforce fear, however. When someone learns that they receive sympathy for being afraid, they may repeat the pattern . . . and become dependent upon externals (someone else giving them attention) to create temporary happiness. This is also true with rewarding yourself to calm away fears. While it may temporarily soothe your emotions, turning to externals such as alcohol, drugs, shopping, and media only reinforces the fear habit.

The path of love is a clear remembrance of God's peace, love, and safety, which is the most calming way to eradicate fears. When you feel afraid, say the name of God repeatedly aloud or in your mind, to soothe and comfort yourself.

Contrast this gentle and effective approach with the ego's path of "conquering fears" by purposely immersing yourself in a frightening situation. This is unnecessary, and only reinforces the belief that fears are necessary and impactful.

The "exhilaration" of the experience of a frightening movie, roller coaster, relationship drama, or other stunt is the experience of your physical body exerting coping mechanisms. The increase in your heart rate and breathing may seem entertaining, yet we are witnessing a physical body in distress. These coping mechanisms were designed to give you strength and energy to escape real physical danger. To your physical body, you *are* in danger in these scenarios, and it responds in kind. This is why you may consider peace to be boring or unattainable.

Similarly, worry is also the sport of the ego. This is the effect of deciding that it's somehow dangerous to be happy, or that "bad follows good." The ego never drops its guard, for fear of perceived danger overtaking its control. And those who listen to the ego's tyrannical dictates are forever caught in the grip of worry and tension.

You can follow the ego, which promises future happiness, or be with God in forever here-and-now happiness. You have the power to decide, now and always.

Your Energy Levels

God is pure energy, and in fact is the *only* energy. God's energy is uplifting, and when you focus upon your oneness with others, you feel uplifted.

With your God-consciousness, you have unlimited access to as much energy as you need. Your four bodies—physical, emotional, energetic, and intellectual—are all affected by whether you're on the path of love or fear.

When you focus upon any aspect of fear—such as believing that there's a lack of what you need; that you're in danger; that other people are separate and are competing with you; that your Source is outside of yourself and must be controlled, chased, or caught—you will notice the energetic effect upon your bodies.

Signs that you're on the *fear* path:

- Physical body feels tense, sore, or ill.
- Emotional body feels anxious, worried, angry, or depressed.
- Intellectual body feels unable to focus.
- Energetic body feels drained and tired.

These signs aren't criticisms; they are your internal feedback of whether you're focusing upon love or fear. Being aware of the signs helps you to read your own energy signals, and decide whether to continue upon the path of love or fear.

Now let us contrast how your four bodies react to your focus upon love—such as seeing the goodness within yourself and others, cooperating instead of competing, having faith in prayers being answered, and allowing yourself to feel happy.

Signs that you're on the *love* path:

- Physical body feels relaxed, healthy, and balanced.

- Emotional body feels peaceful and fulfilled.

- Intellectual body feels able to concentrate and filled with creative ideas and solutions.

- Energetic body feels appropriately energized.

God's energy fuels you naturally, because your natural self *is* God's energy. While the ego believes that the source of energy is external (caffeine, sugar, excitement, or another artificial stimulant), your true self is already energized.

The ego also has a pattern of trying to go faster, in order to reach external goals and accomplishments that it believes will yield happiness and approval. So the ego believes that the key to happiness involves chemically induced energy to help it achieve its unattainable goal of externally derived happiness. The ego is always looking to the future, in order to feel happy now. Yet it makes no sense to have a future orientation to achieve a current status.

In spiritual truth, you are currently and continuously plugged in to God, the Source. You are comfortably nestled within the folds of God's mind right now, and you have everything that you need. There is no need to push, chase, or rush toward anything. Your true self knows that you are already happy and peaceful.

It is in dropping the external chase that internal peace is found. It is in being still within this moment and realizing your oneness with God. The "prize" of life has already been found. All the respect, achievements, accolades, and approval are already yours.

You have helped others by helping yourself to awaken from the dream of separation and lack. Now, go forth and teach through your living example of true and lasting peace and happiness. Be an angel everywhere you go by extending kindness and compassion.

Afterword

Your Mission, Your Livelihood, and Your Beingness

The true meaning of *oneness* is literal. Everyone you see is *you*. So, when someone annoys or angers you, it's an opportunity for you to forgive yourself. This may seem hard to believe, but we are fast-forwarding you to the ultimate spiritual-enlightenment knowledge.

Today, practice forgiving yourself every time you are angered by someone else.

You can say, "Oh, there is me being hurtful."

"Oh, here I am, being dishonest."

And conversely: "Oh, there I am, being successful."

"There I am, being really talented."

"Here I am, being loving."

Everything you see in others is in you as well. As you forgive yourself for everything, you dismantle the illusion of separation. This is how you heal the world.

Giving and *receiving* are not arrows going out from you and arrows coming back, pointing in separate directions. Rather, they are a continuous circle *from* you and *to* you—a vortex—because giving and receiving are one.

Imagine yourself with a spring around you, like a coil of light. This coil is the representation of how the energy of giving and receiving looks. If you only give, the coil will be short. If you allow yourself to receive *and* give, the coil will be long.

Be assured that everything you give to others is identical to giving it to yourself. As you trust in the infinite supply and malleable nature of matter, you live in the comfort of love . . . and so does everyone you encounter.

It's a waste of time and energy to try to change and fix *outward* experiences. Put your whole focus upon making your *inner* world experience abundant, healthy, loving, and peaceful—and that is what your outward experience will be, automatically.

Your life is a dream, and you are the dreamer who controls the direction of your dream. If you ever feel stuck or afraid, call upon we angels to gently awaken you from the dream of fear. We will remind you of the absolute power God created within you. We will teach and show you how to exercise your power of choice and intention.

There are no advantages or "points" that you earn through suffering. There is no one making you do anything, nor are there any blocks or tests. All are freewill choices before you now.

This does require you to create quiet time in which you can honestly interview yourself to decide: *What experience do I desire?*

Since you now know that there is no point in focusing upon acquiring externals, your earthly time and energy can be focused upon enjoying, and sharing the fruits of, your internal world.

You are a spiritual teacher and healer sharing this viewpoint of love, and the positive ripple effects are enormous. As long as you aren't still striving to reach some external "prize," you can be sure that your life of sharing will be one of deep fulfillment and meaning.

We will always clearly guide you according to God's will for your purpose and mission, and help you supply your needs. The pathway, as God intends it for you and your spiritual family, is peaceful.

May you accept peace as your mission, your livelihood, and your beingness. May you choose love as your outlook and the basis for all actions. And may you be as comfortable with your happiness as you once were with misery.

This is our prayer for you, Dear One. And all prayers are answered and fulfilled.

About the Author

Doreen Virtue holds B.A., M.A., and Ph.D. degrees in counseling psychology and is a lifelong sensitive intuitive and Christian mystic. A former psychotherapist, Doreen now gives online workshops on topics related to her books and oracle cards. She's the author of *The Courage to Be Creative, Don't Let Anything Dull Your Sparkle, The Miracles of Archangel Michael*, and *Archangel Oracle Cards*, among many other works. She has appeared on *Oprah*, CNN, the BBC, *The View*, and *Good Morning America* and has been featured in newspapers and magazines worldwide. For information on Doreen's work, please visit her at AngelTherapy.com or Facebook.com/DoreenVirtue444. To enroll in Doreen's video courses, please visit www.HayHouseU.com and www.EarthAngel.com.

ANGEL THERAPY®

✿ ✿ ✿

Hay House Titles of Related Interest

We hope you enjoyed this Hay House book. If you'd like to receive our online catalog featuring additional information on Hay House books and products, or if you'd like to find out more about the Hay Foundation, please contact:

Hay House, Inc., P.O. Box 5100, Carlsbad, CA 92018-5100
(760) 431-7695 or (800) 654-5126
(760) 431-6948 (fax) or (800) 650-5115 (fax)
www.hayhouse.com® • www.hayfoundation.org

Published and distributed in Australia by: Hay House Australia Pty. Ltd., 18/36 Ralph St., Alexandria NSW 2015 • *Phone:* 612-9669-4299 *Fax:* 612-9669-4144 • www.hayhouse.com.au

Published and distributed in the United Kingdom by: Hay House UK, Ltd., Astley House, 33 Notting Hill Gate, London W11 3JQ *Phone:* 44-20-3675-2450 • *Fax:* 44-20-3675-2451 • www.hayhouse.co.uk

Published and distributed in the Republic of South Africa by: Hay House SA (Pty), Ltd., P.O. Box 990, Witkoppen 2068 info@hayhouse.co.za • www.hayhouse.co.za

Published in India by: Hay House Publishers India, Muskaan Complex, Plot No. 3, B-2, Vasant Kunj, New Delhi 110 070 *Phone:* 91-11-4176-1620 • *Fax:* 91-11-4176-1630 • www.hayhouse.co.in

Distributed in Canada by: Raincoast Books, 2440 Viking Way, Richmond, B.C. V6V 1N2 • *Phone:* 1-800-663-5714 *Fax:* 1-800-565-3770 • www.raincoast.com

Take Your Soul on a Vacation

Visit www.HealYourLife.com® to regroup, recharge, and reconnect with your own magnificence. Featuring blogs, mind-body-spirit news, and life-changing wisdom from Louise Hay and friends.

Visit www.HealYourLife.com today!